A Master Guide to PUBLIC SPEAKING

A Master Guide to

PUBLIC SPEAKING

Robert L. Montgomery

HARPER & ROW, PUBLISHERS

New York   Hagerstown   Philadelphia   San Francisco   London

Ann Lander's excerpt on p. 114 courtesy of Publishers-Hall Syndicate.

Senior Production Manager: Kewal K. Sharma
Compositor: VAF House of Typography Ltd.
Printer and Binder: The Maple Press Company

A Master Guide to Public Speaking

Library of Congress Cataloging in Publication Data

Montgomery, Robert Leo, Date—
   A master guide to public speaking.

   Includes index.
   1. Public speaking.   I.   Title.
PN4121.M585   808.5'1   78-19078
ISBN 0-06-044574-2

Contents

Preface

For the first time in American history public speaking courses are in demand. In the past schools offered the subject as an elective. Few students ever signed up for the training; most students avoided these courses out of fear, and completed their formal education without any training in the art of public speaking. A brief anecdote highlights this fear of speaking to a group of any size.

> A king in ancient times became provoked with one of his subjects. He demanded that the subject be tossed to a hungry lion. As the lion approached to devour him, the man spoke to the lion. The lion retreated and left the man alone and alive.
>
> The king was stunned. He shouted, "Bring that man to me! He must be a prophet!" He was brought to the king and His Highness inquired, "What power did you have over the lion? What did you say to the lion?" The man answered, "I simply told the lion that if it ate me, after it finished its dinner it would have to give a speech."

But times are changing fast. What's happening now can be called "open camera" and "open mike," because nothing is hidden anymore. Any day you can have a group of reporters or TV people swoop down on you to question you about your political leanings, company, unemployment, pollution, hiring, poverty, or even toothpaste or breakfast cereal preference.

When the press come into a company or organization to get answers, often the people who have to answer have never been trained to speak as representatives of the company. Often the company's image deteriorates because the people give ungrammatical and unclear statements or answers to the reporters. Some of these films or recordings are played many times to the listening or viewing audience.

Corporations are finally realizing the power of the press to promote or damage their image. One TV authority has figured out that more people watch one program on a third or fourth rated TV station in a city of 1 million than heard St. Paul the Apostle preach in his entire career.

We are living in an age when it is in vogue to speak up for your rights, to praise the good and correct the bad. It is no longer American to let fear, shyness, inhibition, nervousness, or butterflies curb your ability to speak out for what is right and just. Your vote in the quiet of the voting booth is the first step. Next is your assertiveness in making sure promises are kept, laws aren't broken, and our freedom is preserved.

Cicero said 100 years before Christ, "It is reason and speech that unite men to one another; there is nothing else in which we differ so entirely from the brute creation." And William James once remarked, "The meaning of life is to spend it for something more important than self." Being able to express yourself effectively will help to make that possible.

This book is dedicated to helping you perfect the art of public speaking so you can become your most confident and natural self. Remember, the ability to speak effectively is an acquirement, not a gift.

Robert L. Montgomery

What This Master Guide Can Do for You

This guide can change your life. Leadership and success come faster to those who can express themselves effectively. I am going to reveal the secrets of the masters for dynamic public speaking. For 35 years I have pursued a career of platform speaking, including 30 years of work in radio broadcasting and 25 years in TV. I have decided to share the tricks and techniques I've learned from top professional speakers and trainers as well as teachers, professors, and businesspeople. I am making available to you in this book the methods I learned the hard way from speaking and teaching in corporations, universities, and organizations. You will also profit from the innovative and original ideas I've gained from the more than 100,000 men and women I've personally trained in persuasive platform speaking. I will uncover all the shortcuts I've learned from 35 years of solid professional public speaking experience. These tips will help you to get your ideas expressed, accepted, and acted upon.

Although I have made thousands of speeches over the years, I still have some butterflies and feelings of tension and anxiety before I make a speech. I have noted that most top speakers have similar feelings. However, we have learned a number of invaluable secrets for controlling this tension and making it work for us. Chapter 1 reveals to you the professional techniques used by the masters. Just about every individual is interested in becoming more confident, more professional, and more successful. Also in Chapter 1, I share the methods for gaining confidence and authority in communicating to groups and I make available the tricks for making your voice and delivery more professional. By learning and practicing these techniques you will develop the ability to provide dynamic leadership in your job, at home, and in your community.

Organization is the siamese twin of delivering speeches. Chapter 2 details the master methods of professional speakers for quicker and easier preparation: how they analyze their audience, pick their topic, and select their illustrations, anecdotes, and facts for a winning presentation. In Chapter 3 I discuss how to organize a speech and provide classic kinds of openings and closings I've found to be most successful and most used by top speakers.

Most executives want to know how to sell their ideas upward in management and elsewhere in life. In Chapter 3, I will tell you the master keys for gathering and arranging your evidence to make a persuasive, convincing impact. In our TV era I find that it's essential to know the professional methods for using audiovisual aids. Proper use of visual aids helps to demonstrate effectively your ideas and to exhibit your evidence. In Chapter 4 I present the methods of the modern professionals for perfecting the use of visual aids: what kind to use, when to use them, when not to use them, how many to use, and the key qualities of a good visual aid.

In Chapter 5 I make available to you my own personal secrets for a masterful delivery along with the best methods of the professionals on the international speaking circuit. Since I have taught memory for 25 years, I will tell you how to remember without memorizing, how to use an outline as the professionals do, techniques for timing, 12 practice secrets, and how the professionals involve the audience.

One speciality I've enjoyed teaching speakers and teachers around the world is how to be eloquent in impromptu situations, so I've included in Chapter 6 the secrets for giving successful impromptu talks. You will be given four methods to organize instantly on any topic, key steps to assure instant confidence, pitfalls to avoid, and tips on how to practice for these impromptu challenges.

Another frequent area in which impromptu speaking is necessary is answering questions from a group at a meeting or from an audience following a speech. Chapter 7 provides 11 ways to answer questions professionally before any audience, including a press conference or a congressional inquiry. Hecklers can pop up anywhere these days, so I will tell you how to handle them like the professionals do. Also, I will share the ways in which you can anticipate questions and answer objections. You'll develop an alertness for the unexpected as well as an ability to perform better in meetings, discussions, and conferences.

One of my hobbies over the years and a speciality in any speaking has been the art of using humor. It has been a difficult, up-hill fight for me to develop this ability as my initial and long-time success was in giving serious speeches. Yet, what I learned by befriending and studying top comedians enabled me to find out the secrets of this art. The techniques I mastered are so effective that I was able to win three first-place awards for humorous speaking in 1976 alone. I want you to learn these techniques. They are included in Chapter 8 along with topics such as when not to use humor, why and how to use humor, the best kinds of humorous material and where to find it. I also provide guidelines for being a humorous toastmaster or master-of-ceremonies.

My experience includes more than 3000 hours of interviewing celebrities and interesting people on radio and TV. In Chapter 9 I will tell you the do's and don't's of using a microphone and facing a camera. In our era of film and TV I feel you will benefit by knowing also how to prepare and how to rehearse for a filming or for a TV show. Also included are professional tips on using the proper language and avoiding traits of an amateur.

Many of us in all levels of management and in all types of community, professional, religious, and educational organizations are called on occasionally to chair a meeting, present an award, introduce a speaker, give a report, or receive a gift or an award. In Chapter 10 I will cover all the special occasions for speech-making one by one and tell you how best to be professional in the assignment. Chapter 11 will tell you how to save time and get better results in meetings, conferences and discussions. I will tell you how to be a successful moderator or chairperson and how to be an effective participant.

You will find that leadership becomes easier as you learn to speak more vitally, convincingly, and professionally. Therefore, I have provided a complete index of model openings and closings, humorous anedcotes, one-liners. clever speech lines and patter, and stirring illustrations to help you in gathering colorful material. You'll find this resource material in Chapter 12.

My objective beyond creating a quick and easy guide to professional public speaking is to help you develop a new enthusiasm for speaking from a platform. Also, I feel that your new confidence will help you become a more sparkling conversationalist.

This handy guide will also make it easy for you to improve youself in many other essential areas such as appearance, gestures, making introductions, gaining a rapport, and developing your own style. It took me many years to learn the right way to do all of these things more quickly and more professionally. You'll gain them in the time it takes to read this guide. And I know you will no longer fear public speaking once you've read this guide; in fact, I feel certain that you will begin to find it a pleasure to speak to groups of all sizes—from 10 to 10,000.

You will also discover that you can speak more confidently, convincingly, and colorfully after you've finished reading this guide because the techniques that fill it are proven methods of the top professionals. Besides, they are easy to learn and apply, since they are specific, clear, and simple. I will tell you the methods that work best and provide illustrations to explain where and how to use them. You will also become a more positive thinker and doer once you practice and acquire these habits.

The ideas, examples, and secrets included in this guide are the result of 35 years in the communication business. I include the lessons I've learned from professionals as well as my own techniques developed since making my first public speech in 1939. I feel you will learn more and learn quickly from these methods because I can do what I teach. In fact, I do speak professionally and also teach men and women of all ages how to speak.

Helping people to learn to speak effectively can be compared to a jeweler polishing a gem. The grinding and cutting add nothing to the jewel; they only reveal the wealth within.

You'll find this guide to be a practical, plain-talking book that tells you how to master the art of dynamic public speaking and uncover the wealth of talent you possess. You will now have at your fingertips one comprehensive reference guide to help you become confident and professional in prepared or impromptu speaking to groups of any size.

A Master Guide to PUBLIC SPEAKING

CHAPTER 1

Secrets of Professional Speakers

THREE SECRETS OF PERSUASIVE COMMUNICATION

What do you think of when you hear the word "communications"—television, radio, and miles and miles of telephone wire and cable? That's the usual answer. That's why I have taken the "*s*" off the end of the word and made it singular, "communication." Now it's a different word, isn't it, and you think of public speaking or effective speaking person to person.

The top rung on the ladder of business success is defined by many management consultants, including myself, as "the ability to communicate." We can define a leader as one who draws or directs by influence; directs an action, thought, or opinion; makes a beginning; moves in advance of; takes initiative; or shows the way. Success as a leader depends on one's ability to lead, guide, or direct others through the effective communication of ideas.

Bernard Baruch observed, "The ability to express an idea is well nigh as important as the idea itself." Finally, Cicero's statement points the way to becoming an effective speaker, "The skill to do comes from doing."

One question I am asked more than any other in my speaking and teaching engagements around the country is, "How do you sell an idea?" In other words, how do you persuade and convince upper management to approve of your requests? A simple answer is, "Prepare a case for yourself and your needs." A more detailed answer is to consider the three great secrets of persuasive communication: (1) what you say and how you say it; (2) what you do and how you do it; and (3) what you think and why you think it. Oral communication includes all three. After all, we're never just saying a few words; we're always revealing a human personality—ideas, words, thoughts, feelings, behavior, and example.

This concept is so important that I want to explain here Aristotle's three secrets for persuading others. He called them *logos, pathos,* and *ethos. Logos* is logical proof: the kind of ideas, evidence, arguments, and reasoning that we associate with court cases. It is the proof that resides in the speech itself (explained in detail in Chapter 3).

Pathos is emotional proof: linking ideas in a speech with the needs and desires of the audience. Thus, it is the proof that resides within the audience. I have devoted part of Chapter 2 to how to analyze an audience.

Ethos is ethical proof. This is the most potent of the three means of persuasion. It is the proof that resides within the speaker. The audience will accept the ideas in a speech on the basis of who the person is making the speech. This acceptance can be based on the reputation of the speaker or it can be created during the speech by the speaker's personality and the ideas presented. The ethical proof for persuasion can be created through the speaker's words and actions if the listeners are convinced that the speaker has all three of these qualities: intelligence, goodwill, and integrity. Intelligence in this instance consists of logic and common sense as well as I.Q. The speaker possesses goodwill if it is demonstrated that the listeners' best interests have been considered. And integrity is earned if the listeners see the speaker as a good person. Of these three qualities necessary in a speaker for ethical proof, integrity is the most persuasive. Aristotle summed it up in this thought: "Character is the most effective agent of persuasion."

The question is, how can you be sure that you possess these qualities when you are facing the audience? The answer is that it starts with attitude.

DEVELOPING THE KEY QUALITIES OF A SUCCESSFUL SPEECH

The essence of a good speech is that a speaker really has something to say and really wants to say it. You must feel you have something to say that people should hear. This requires a positive attitude about your subject and its importance. You can develop this positive attitude by preparation through study or experience. In fact, your selection of the appropriate topic often can determine your success more than your ability as a speaker.

Also, your attitude towards yourself is important. You should like yourself and have confidence in your ability to speak to a group of any size. And you should have a positive attitude about the audience: you should feel that they will like you. The audience readily can sense from your voice, body language, and example whether or not you are confident, you believe what you say, and you like them or not. It has been stated correctly that there are no bad audiences, only poor speakers.

"Alright, that's fine," you may say, "but how do I develop this positive attitude?" By preparation and practice. In fact, the more you practice, the more confident and positive you'll become. Preparation breeds confidence, and practice does indeed make one more perfect in the art of public speaking. The skill to do comes from doing. And the more you practice, the easier the doing becomes.

Looking your best is another way you can build a positive attitude. Of course, I am referring to appearance, the image you present to others. This includes your dress, your posture, and your facial expressions. Avoiding extremes of dress and manner will help assure an attitude of confidence towards yourself. Neatness counts: clean your fingernails and shoes; keep your hair trimmed; have your clothes pressed. The objective is to get your message across clearly to your audience. Try to present an appearance that doesn't detract from this objective.

Total grooming is a concept of the late 1970s; it includes a complete coordination of clothing colors with shoes, hair, and makeup. Don't overlook a warm, natural smile. Most speakers are too serious. They may be happy but they fail to notify their face. Also, posture can communicate vitality or laziness. Whether you remain seated or standing, keep your posture alive and erect.

Personality is the impression we convey to others: what we say, how we look, and what we do. It is also what others think about us. Dr. Henry C. Link observed, "Personality is the extent to which the individual has developed habits and skills which interest and serve other people." Therefore, developing a strong personality includes being interested in others and developing skills that can be used to serve others.

In summary, the key qualities for a successful speech are choosing a topic about which you feel deeply, preparing thoroughly, presenting a positive mental attitude, and showing an interest in your audience by a neat appearance and a friendly voice.

An old saying suggests, "What you are speaks so loudly I can't hear what you say." Our behavior, our example communicates a great deal about us whether we talk or not. As the poet Edgar Guest said, "I'd rather see a sermon any day than hear one."

ESSENTIAL GUIDES OF BEHAVIOR

We are communicating all the time, through our gestures, our eyes, our facial expressions, posture, and tone of voice. All of these are types of body language that communicate something about us to others. That's why, as a wise professor once declared, "People catch more than they learn." That is, our behavior, our example becomes the real teacher.

In India a teacher is known as a *guru*. One definition of a guru is: "Behavior manifests belief." Or, in other words, actions speak louder than words. So try to avoid facial ticks, slouchy posture, flagrant gestures, or worse, no gestures. Avoid speaking in a monotone or constantly shouting. Neither be a statue nor a windmill; neither be a geyser nor a mud puddle. In short, be aware of your behavior as well as your appearance. Be a good guru and practice what you preach for best results. Don't allow a gap between the spoken word and the example. Always be honest. Be yourself at your best.

Abraham Lincoln once said, "When I see a person talk, I like to see them talk as though they're fighting a swarm of bees." Effective speaking is the result of a deep and abiding desire to share your ideas with your listeners, but it takes energy and animation to convey conviction. Quoting William Jennings Bryan, "It is necessary to have something more than knowledge of the subject. You must have earnestness in its presentation. You must feel that you have something to say that people ought to hear."

HOW PROFESSIONALS CONTROL TENSION

It is natural for speakers to have some tension and nervousness when they appear before an audience. Most professional speakers confess to having anxiety or butterflies when they are going to give a speech. Perhaps that's the reason the orator Cicero said many years ago, "All speaking of merit is characterized by nervousness." The way to handle this tension is to put it to work for you; get into action. Action cures nervousness. Let your hands be free by your sides. Just as naturally as in everyday conversation, you will gesture appropriately. Don't lock your hands behind your back, put them in your pockets, or clasp them in front of you. Keep them by your side when they're not in action. As Hamlet said to the actors, ". . . suit the words to the action, the action to the words."

There are only a few known ways to control fear. The first is to admit it. We can't cure what we won't recognize as a problem. Next, as Ralph Waldo Emerson suggested, "Do the thing you fear and the death of fear is certain." So, again, practice as much as you possibly can. There's no better antidote for fear or tension than action. A well-prepared speech is more easily presented. Also, the minute before you're going to speak, take a couple of deep breaths. This will help you get the butterflies in formation and also will give you control of your voice. Poise is control of your emotions, including your voice. Another tip is to take a sip or two of water or any nonalcoholic liquid, hot or cold. It will keep your throat and mouth moist so that you won't choke or cough. Tension can cause a dry throat and add to your nervousness as well as freeze your voice.

Other professional techniques for controlling fear include giving yourself a pep talk before you are introduced. In her book *Wake Up and Live* Dorothea Brande suggests, "Prepare, then act as though it were impossible to fail." If you tell yourself to act enthusiastic, you'll be enthusiastic, or to act confident, and you'll be confident. Tell yourself that this is your chance to inspire, inform, or convince others. Now get excited. Act alive, think alive, talk alive!

A pep talk is merely a positive mental reflection; it tells you to have faith in yourself. Most individuals know their faults quite well, but they do not have a true appreciation of their uniqueness, their individual positive traits, or their abilities.

Physical exercise will help you get physically in shape for your talk. Walking briskly around the block once or twice will help a great deal. Some speakers, do simple arm exercises or bends. Any physical movement will help ease anxiety.

Prayer helps many control their nervousness. A prayerful reflection can provide an aura of calm about you.

You now have a choice of methods with which to combat tension. Put your anxiety to work for you. Develop the attitude of a winner. It can bring out the best in you if you put it to work for you. Get into action. Use gestures or visual aids such as charts or graphs to provide purposeful movement for you—movement that will help you channel your tension.

PROFESSIONAL VOICE TECHNIQUES

The human voice is an amazing thing; it starts working the moment you're born and doesn't stop until you stand up to speak in public. Stage fright is commonplace. Few speakers are free of voice or nervous tension, wet palms, or butterflies in the stomach. Tension is a good thing only if you put it to work for you.

Olympic champions, in fact all athletes and performers, know that without some anxiety or nervousness to use to their advantage, they won't do as well. The person who is utterly lacking in nervousness before an audience quite often is a dull speaker. Do as the professionals have done: develop the habit of courage by confronting fear.

Voice improvement or delivery begins with an appreciation of the need for enthusiasm, energy, and animation: in a nutshell, vitality of voice, posture, and spirit. The dictionary definition of *vitality* gives us an insight into why it is an essential quality: it is "the characteristic that distinguishes the living from the nonliving." We need a subject we can sink our teeth into. Mastery in the subject will help you project greater vitality. Remember, everyone is eloquent enough in what he knows.

Knowing your subject matter thoroughly and using an outline will cure the stage fright that causes loss of voice and will also provide you with a reserve of poise and confidence. Know more about your topic than you'll have time to tell. This will assure you a dynamic conviction and more material for the question and answer session that often follows.

Some psychologists feel that the voice is second only to facial expression in influencing others. Our voice is the main instrument we have for communication with people. The late H. L. Hunt, one of the richest men in America, spent hundreds of thousands of dollars in radio advertising for over 1400 products in his company. He said his reason for doing this was, "because the human voice from an unseen source is the most effective agent of persuasion." Not just any voice is effective, however, but a pleasant voice, strong, ringing melodiously with conviction or sincerity.

All of us are sensitive to sound. Invest in a tape recorder and record yourself. Play it back and listen to yourself. When you evaluate a recording of your voice, rate yourself (or have others rate you) according to this checklist:

Is your voice rough or smooth?
Is your voice cheerful or complaining?
Is your speech too fast or too slow?
Is your voice too high or too low?
Is your speech monotonous or just right?
Is your vocal style stimulating or boring?

Follow the example of actor Don Ameche and his brother Jim—put a smile in your voice. A mental attitude of joy contributes to a happy, pleasant, modulated voice.

Try to avoid nasality or talking through your nose. It's a lazy way of speaking. Get excited and avoid listlessness. It's hard work to speak well anytime but especially when you address a group, so put life into your voice. Avoid being strident or talking in a high-strung, high-pitched voice. Be careful not to mumble, ramble, babble, or swallow words and sentence endings. Try not to be loud or harsh. Don't speak with an upbraiding voice. We should remember Abe Lincoln's response when his mother asked him after a highly emotional church sermon, "Did you enjoy the sermon?" Abe shook his head and said, "No, ma'am, I didn't. The preacher talked so loud I couldn't hear him."

Practice is the best way to improve the pitch, projection, pauses, emphasis, or pace in your voice. Reading a newspaper or magazine out loud, to yourself, or others can help you improve your voice and develop a personal style of speaking. Try to read with feeling and interpret the content with emphasis, as a newscaster or announcer would do on radio or TV. This kind of practice will help you improve the natural resonance of your voice as well as the art of speaking. Your vocal chords will strengthen automatically. Try to practice doing this an hour every day. Split the time into two or three sessions.

Take deep breaths. Breathe from your diaphragm, the lower stomach region. This will give you voice power for greater projection and emphasis. It will improve your breath control and enable you to increase your pace, the ability to slow down when you are establishing a point or to speed up when providing less essential material.

Pace is the characteristic of a speech that separates the amateurs from the professionals. The ability to speed up or slow down at appropriate times to keep the speech lively is what professional speakers are paid for. Their fees range from $1000 to $4000 for a one-hour talk. Paul Harvey, a news commentator and professional speaker is one of the professionals in this category. You can study his delivery—the art of faster and slower pace—weekdays on the ABC radio news network. (He is usually on at noon and again at around 6 to 7 P.M.) He is a masterful speaker. His fine style is obvious even on radio when he works from a script.

As a speech teacher for many years, I've had to slow down only 1 speaker in every 100. I've had to build a fire under the other 99. When an individual is new to public speaking or teaching, it is difficult for that individual to know when he or she is projecting enough. Many people feel it is phony to show emotion or enthusiasm, yet it takes emotion and enthusiasm to put ideas across successfully to a group.

Often it is difficult to get people to be enthusiastic enough. It's a natural reaction for you to feel that you're being too forceful, but it takes much more force and feeling, as well as firm gestures, to convince an audience. The one, deep obligation of any speaker, anytime, anywhere, even on the telephone is to be audible, to be heard with ease. This takes speech power. If the audience is falling asleep during the talk, the problem is with the speaker's vitality. Zsa Zsa Gabor once replied to reporters who remarked that she had a lot of men in her life, "Frankly, I prefer *life* in my men!" Audiences prefer *life* in all speakers, men or women, young or old.

Also, over the years I've had to quiet down only about 1 speaker in every 100. Occasionally, a speaker speaks loudly all the time, and it becomes necessary to teach that speaker modulation of the voice, that is, softer intensity.

Making a point with softer intensity at times is a professional trait. An entire speech can be whispered if it is done with enough intensity. Too many people speak so softly in their presentations that they cannot be heard. People will respond quickly to a whisper, but the words must be audible; listeners should not have to strain to hear them. Stand up to be seen. Speak up to be heard. Sit down to be loved.

When you read for practice or speak from memory, try always to use a tape recorder or, if possible, a video recorder so you can see as well as hear yourself. And try to get someone to listen to you and give you feedback. It's difficult to know how you're coming across without being able to hear yourself or without a listener to tell you.

As you speak, bring key words, adjectives, and verbs to life. For clarity, it is necessary to highlight key words and phrases with feeling and emphasis. Meanings of ideas change as vocal emphasis changes. I could say "I detest you," yet sound seductive, simply through vocal emphasis. The voice is versatile if it is used properly.

Some speakers don't pause enough and therefore don't allow listeners time to assimilate the ideas spoken. Practice pausing as you read. Almost any classical stories from literature lend themselves to being read out loud: nursery rhymes, riddles, and stories for children or adults. Read them with feeling or even act them out dramatically for practice. Have other family members do the same. Be competitive by recording them and voting on a winner.

Practice pauses, emphasis, pitch (higher and lower vocal ranges), force (loudness and softness) and pace (faster and slower). Chapter 5 will discuss further the methods of practicing the speeches you'll be giving. A final point on voice. To avoid monotony when you are speaking, get excited about your topic and your audience and put more life into your speaking. Instead of being tight-jawed, as so many speakers are, open your mouth wide and speak from the diaphragm, the lower abdomen. Speak up and out. By simply opening your mouth wide to the size of a half-dollar and projecting, you will eliminate nasality, poor articulation, and inaudibility.

CHAPTER 2

Master Methods for Preparing Presentations

ANALYZING THE AUDIENCE

Questions the Professionals Ask

This chapter and Chapter 3 are designed to help you achieve excellence in speech content and organization. This is half of speaking; the other half has to do with delivery. Where does one begin? What comes first?

Let's look at it from the point of view of the *audience*. There are three kinds of speakers: those you listen to; those you can't listen to; and those you can't help listening to. The first step towards developing an arresting speech is to begin your preparation by analyzing the audience you'll be addressing. Audience analysis is the most overlooked fundamental in public speaking.

Even before you pick a topic you should analyze the audience you'll be influencing. You can't tailor your communication until you know precisely who you'll be talking to. Some questions the professionals ask include:

What does my audience have in common?
Is the audience made up of men or women, or both?
How many people are in the audience?
What is the average age?
What is their background: education, religion, special interests?
Why are they coming to listen to me?
How much do they know already about the topic I have chosen?
How much more do they need to know about this topic?
What attitudes will they bring with them?
What do I want to accomplish?

Every speaker should decide what specific type of speech he or she will present. Will it be a speech to inform, entertain, convince, persuade, or perhaps stir the listeners to take a definite action? This decision is a most important one.

HOW TO AVOID SELECTING THE WRONG TOPIC

Success in public speaking is more certain if you always consider the "don'ts" of selecting a topic.

Don't underestimate the intelligence of your listeners.
Never overestimate your listeners' need for information and clarification through examples or illustrations.
Don't use jargon, slang, or "inside" terminology; nothing loses an audience faster than terms they don't understand.

There are a few "do's" you should consider.

Always define your terms, especially acronyms, formulas, and abbreviations. (The greatest enemy of communication is the illusion of it. There are 500 common words used in everyday English that have over 14,000 dictionary definitions. This means that each word has about 28 definitions. So always define your key terms or ideas.)
Illustrate your points. This provides your audience with greater clarity and understanding.
Try to understand the problems and personal interests of your audience.
Gain an awareness of the situation, the occasion, and the environment.

Other questions that professionals ask include, "Will the speech take place before or after a meal?" "Is a serious or informal talk expected?" "Will I be speaking early or late in the program?" "At what time of day will I be speaking?" "Will I be speaking in a small room or a large hall?" These questions will help you know what to talk about, what to avoid, and what to emphasize. And the answers to these questions will also help you decide on the overall purpose or objective of your speech: the one dominant idea or purpose you have decided is best for this audience at this time.

The two most important questions are: "Who are the members of the audience?" and "What should I talk about?" Sometimes the topic will be picked for you. Perhaps a group or organization will ask you to talk about a particular subject. But try always to do an audience analysis first. Even if you are given the topic or subject, it's important to ask yourself all of the questions I've suggested to ensure a successful speech. I always ask the program chairman or sponsor 15 or 20 questions. Once I asked the sponsor who the speakers had been in the past few months and what their topics were. I discovered that the speaker the month before had talked on the same subject I was going to speak about. Of course I then chose an entirely different topic.

Once you've gained some knowledge of the audience makeup and background, you will find it easier to pick a topic and tailor it to that group. However, think about the event and the audience for a few days, or even longer if possible. In time, a subject will pop into your mind.

When you are given the freedom of selecting the topic, remember that the best speech is a re-creation of a portion of one's life. As the author Rudyard Kipling said, "Ah what avails the classic bent, And what the cultured word; Against the undoctored incident that actually occurred." Or, to repeat Socrates' statement, "Everyone is eloquent enough in what they know."

You are the world's greatest authority on yourself—your goals, beliefs, experiences, values, and convictions. So speak from personal experience. For any topic you choose there are two kinds of preparation, *remote* and *proximate*. *Remote preparation* is everything you've seen, heard, or learned about a subject. And that kind of preparation—what you've carried with you for months or years on a topic—is the best kind of preparation.

An example of remote preparation can be as simple as your thinking about an experience that taught you a lesson or a happy occasion that you'll never forget. For instance, if you have a scar on your hand, you could give an eloquent talk instantly by telling what happened, when it happened, where you were, who was there, why it happened, how it happened, and what you learned from the accident. People want to hear about your experiences first-hand; they want to know what life has taught you, not what you've read in a book and memorized, because that comes second-hand.

The second kind of preparation, *proximate preparation*, covered in Chapter 3, is what you learn and gather on a topic from the time you have been engaged for the speech until you have given it. Both kinds contribute to a solid talk.

HOW TO LIMIT YOUR TOPIC

Once you've selected a topic, you must begin to limit it. Before you put a word on paper, before you utter a word orally, you must limit your topic in your own mind to one dominant theme, suited to the material and the particular audience.

The idea, limited, is of primary importance. Words and illustrations come later. For example, if you decide you would like to give a speech against Communism, it wouldn't help a bit to think that the purpose of your speech is merely to speak against Communism. This is too vague, too general a purpose. It is not limited. But if you analyze the audience, which is the first thing every speaker should do and you see that it is composed of many political and economic types, you might limit the purpose of your speech to showing that Soviet Communism by its basic principles and acts denies the possibility of coexistence with any other form of economic order. As soon as you form this limited purpose, thoughts will begin to flow.

On the other hand, you might analyze the audience and find that it is made up of religious people. Then you might make it your limited purpose to show that Soviet Communism, by its basic principles and acts denies religion and God, and is the first political system in the world to have atheism as its first principle.

As soon as you have a limited purpose, you will find that ideas, suggestions, examples, and sources come to mind. And when you finish your speech, the audience will have what you have: one definite idea in their minds. They will have it because you had one definite idea in mind before you started to speak.

As another example, let us suppose you are planning to talk about communication. But, communication is too general a topic. It is necessary to limit the scope of your topic to get the message across in the time allowed. Remember, the speaker's main purpose is to get the point across clearly. Once you have analyzed the audience and noted that it is composed of teachers, you might decide to limit your purpose to communication through visual aids. Or, if the audience were made up of managers in business, you might limit your purpose to the importance of listening as an essential principle of effective communication.

Limiting your topic is important, but you must also take into consideration that the time you will spend on talking about the topic should also be limited. Often you will be told the time allowed: 20 or 30 minutes, or maybe an hour. Limiting the scope of the subject enables you to keep your speech within the time allowed. Too many speakers talk too long, even trained speakers. It's a common fault. Yet, nothing is more professional than good timing and finishing on time.

I also suggest that you write your purpose out, because writing it will make it more precise. Write it out so you can see it. Put it before you like a bull's-eye.

After you've written out your purpose, thought about your topic, discussed it, read about it, and limited it, you are ready to apply the second rule: selection. You must select the specific material suited to the limited purpose and the particular audience.

I've found that the easiest way to gather material is to write it on 3 × 5 or 4 × 6 cards. Keep them handy in a pocket or purse, by the nightstand, in your library, or on a bookshelf, so that you'll have them when inspiration strikes you or when you come across a quotation or statistic. Just pull out a card and jot down the idea or information you want to remember. You can eventually put the cards in a file box and organize them according to major categories or you can put them in large envelopes and mark the contents on the front.

As an example, I am writing this book based on a lifetime of experience in the speech field, but I couldn't possibly recall all the essentials, quotations, statistics, examples, stories, or facts if I hadn't written them down over a period of time. Consequently, I keep a huge cardboard box filled with envelopes and file folders, meaning that the basic contents of this book are all in one place. The envelopes are marked: organization, preparation, quotes, statistics, and so on. This saves a lot of time—one of the most precious of all commodities.

At this point don't think of the order in which you're going to present your thoughts or of the words that you're going to use. Ideas come to us, usually, in most amazing disorder. Just jot them down as they occur to you and think of only one thing: Does this case, quotation, example, or idea, suit my limited purpose? Does it shoot right at the bull's-eye I have before me? It if does, put it into the file box or envelope; if it doesn't, reject it or put it into a folder marked "miscellaneous." In this way you will gather gradually a number of notes or ideas. When you have enough material, you'll be ready to move on to the next step. But first, you should be aware of some formal as well as informal sources for obtaining suitable content to support your idea.

SOURCES FOR GATHERING MATERIAL

You may have some of the best sources for speech material in your library at home. Also whatever you've saved from school assignments, speeches, themes, term papers, or a thesis are all excellent possibilities for speech content. Even if you don't have some of the books or magazines that I will suggest, your local library will have most of them. In addition you should have two different desk-size dictionaries, because often you can find just the right word or definition by checking two different sources. Make certain the dictionaries are between 800 to 1,600 pages in length. Be sure they are recent editions, if possible, within the last five years. If you can buy a dictionary with sections titled "Biographical Names," "Abbreviations," "Handbook of Style," "Colleges and Universities," in the back it will be an asset. You will find that these sections will come in handy frequently.

Also, buy a thesaurus of synonyms and antonyms in a pocket-size version if you cannot afford the large hardbound. It will be helpful when you are trying to find the right word. Remember what Samuel Clements (Mark Twain) said: "The difference between the right word and the almost right word is the difference between lightning and the lightning bug."

Another excellent aid for finding colorful, convincing, supportive material is *Bartlett's Familiar Quotations* (the shorter version is available in paperback). It will provide a rich and varied treasury of information on every subject at your fingertips, since it contains many passages, phrases, and proverbs traced to their sources in ancient and modern literature. You can find almost any poem or quotation under the author's name or by looking up one key word or phrase. Or you can look up a particular topic and see what has been written about that topic. For example, suppose you wanted to see what is available under "quotations." You would find 14 references just in the shorter version of Bartlett's work. Two of them, both spoken or written by Ralph Waldo Emerson, are almost contradictory. The first is, "I hate quotations. Tell me what you know." The second is, "Next to the originator of a good sentence is the first quoter of it."

Poetry can help you to make a point or get your idea across more colorfully in a speech. A poem also is an excellent way to open or close a speech. A little poetry mixed into the middle of your content can provide clarity as well as variety. I always keep a paperback of Shakespeare's plays nearby along with some small and large editions of poetry. If you're not interested in buying books on poetry, *Bartlett's Familiar Quotations* contains enough reference material to famous poems so that you will at least not ignore this rich possibility for speech content. (If you write your own poetry, buy a rhyming dictionary to help you; it will save you some time.)

Humor is a necessary ingredient in speeches in today's changing, serious, problem-filled world. Besides adding variety, a change of pace, and perhaps a good laugh, it can lightly make an important point.

Bookstores and libraries are filled with inexpensive joke books, as well as small and large editions on humor and humorous stories (see also Chapter 8). I got my newest joke book at the local drugstore for $1.25. Although humor doesn't come naturally to me, it has been a hobby of mine since grade school. I have an extensive collection on the subject. This new paperback is "Don't Put My Name On This Book" by Henny Youngman. Actually, it says, "Anonymously written by Henny Youngman." He is known as the "King of One-Liners." A sample from this new book is, "In Las Vegas, a man walked up to his wife and said, "Give me the money I told you not to give me!" The point one could make with this one-liner is that brevity is the soul of wit and also the soul of clarity.

Other helpful works you should have in your own library or office for finding instant facts, statistics, references, stories, and historical incidents include an encyclopedia, a world almanac, and the Bible. Reader's Digest and the New York Daily News publish annual almanacs. A world atlas might come in handy as well.

Finally, the best sources of all for colorful and convincing material besides your personal experiences are the daily newspapers and current magazines. There is nothing more interesting to people than topical news and current features. The daily paper and current magazines will provide you with up-to-the-minute topics, facts, statistics, and ideas. Your imagination and creativity will do the rest. The sports and comic sections, as well as the front-page and editorial sections, contain the latest happenings.

THE MAGIC OF EXAMPLES

There are at least two excellent reasons for collecting and saving material in file boxes or envelopes and for developing a basic library of the many standard books just listed. The first is so that you will have specific, graphic, memorable material to fill your speeches, for this is your evidence, your supporting data. The second is so that you will have it at hand when you need it without having to wait or search unnecessarily, which can take excessive amounts of time.

The Romans said, "Exemplum docet," which translated means, "The example teaches." And it teaches best. So the secret of effective speaking is the same as that of colorful or convincing writing: fill your talks with examples and illustrations.

Examples come in a variety of forms: statistics, facts, quotations, experiences, illustrations, stories, jokes, anecdotes, expert testimony, or actual incidents. All provide specific, graphic, memorable magic to any talk. Chapter 3 will illustrate how you can arrange these examples once you've gathered them, but a few ideas on using them are necessary here. Following a night on the town by conventioneers, a chairman got immediate attention of the sleepy attendees at 8 A.M. by saying, "You can't soar with the eagles in the morning if you hoot with the owls at night." The quotation drew some hoots, but most members of the audience laughed and instantly became more awake and interested. All it took was one good thought.

I once heard a speaker quote Mark Twain, "There are liars and damn liars; and then there are statistics." I want to illustrate the importance of providing statistics or factual data in speeches to show trends, convince others, or make a point. Without these statistics, facts, or examples, you will fail in your attempts to persuade your audience.

Always try to illustrate the statistic for the sake of clarity and so the audience will understand the meaning of the statistic. For example, suppose in a speech you said that if all the oceans dried up there would be enough salt left to build a wall 180 miles long and 1 mile thick and that such a wall would reach once around the earth at the equator. Or to put it another way, if all the oceans dried up the salt left would have a bulk about 15 times as much as the entire continent of Europe. Don't these statistics illustrate more clearly that there are millions of pounds of salt available in the world than just a simple statement to that effect? These statistics are now meaningful and memorable.

Recently I heard a dairy expert explain how much milk we produce annually in America. Knowing that the raw statistic of so many millions of gallons would only confound the listeners and have little meaning, he explained with an analogy: "If all the milk produced in one year in the United States were put into quart containers, the containers placed end-to-end would extend around the earth 20 times and to the moon and back." The audience gave that speaker an ovation for a stunningly clear statistical fact. He had done his homework.

There aren't a lot of ways to simplify technical or statistical data, but you should try to avoid giving them in a dry, technical, uninteresting way. You'll learn in Chapter 4 how to use visual aids to illustrate statistics with graphs, charts, and slides or with an overhead projector. Visuals are one way to make technical material more interesting and clearer to listeners. Otherwise using the technique of comparison and contrast offers the next best possibility. Some examples follow. Wilbur and Orville Wright made the first airplane flight in 1903. Orville Wright flew 120 feet in 12 seconds. To illustrate how far we've come since then, compare the length of the first flight with the wingspan of a 747: it is longer than the length of the first flight. (In all fairness, however, on that same day in

1903, Wilbur Wright flew 852 feet in 59 seconds on the fourth flight of the day.) Where would you find these facts? In an encyclopedia or a world almanac. Of course, the comparison is the key to illustrating it. Or, to explain in an interesting way that there are 22 million citizens in Canada you could say that the state of California has almost as many people living in it as does the entire country of Canada—22 million.

Sometimes statistics can provide a startling opening for a speech, as you will learn in Chapter 3. As an example, I once heard a speaker grab the attention of an audience with this opening: "There are more abortions in Washington, D.C., the nation's capital, than there are births. And New York isn't far behind; there are four abortions for every five births recorded in New York City."

It is always advisable to substantiate facts and statistics. The more recent the statistic is, of course, the stronger is the evidence. Always save the record of where you got the information and include the date as well. More and more speakers and writers are being asked to corroborate their evidence.

Facts can make a provocative opening as well. For instance, a reporter posed a question to an audience this way: "How is it that in the state of Pennsylvania, a 16-year-old girl can get an abortion without her parents' consent but needs their permission to get her ears pierced?" The reporter didn't have an answer, and the audience didn't have an answer either, but the question served as an attention-getter.

Sometimes analogies can be strengthened. In the opening of a speech I heard recently the speaker promised to show the audience how to save 25 percent on their water bills and included this fact: a faucet dripping one drip continually for one year will waste 700 gallons of water. He added, "That's enough water to fill three waterbeds." It would have been better had he given the cost of 700 wasted gallons of water and said how badly the water is needed in some regions.

In mid-1977 a raging controversy took place over whether the Concorde, a supersonic transport, should be allowed to land at JFK Airport in New York City. Britain and France were pushing for the rights to land the plane there. People who live near the airfield, as well as the governor of New York, were up in arms about the possibility and opposed to it. I heard a speaker on TV, who won some votes for the Concorde landing in a unique way. He offered what he termed "misconceptions followed by facts." I was surprised at most of them, especially the first. He said, "Misconception: The Concorde is a giant plane. Fact: The Concorde is a medium-sized jet, about one-third as large as a 747." One after another he exploded myths and gave the facts. His method of delivery was outstanding, and the startling facts definitely won over the audience, who applauded briskly. I felt that much of the applause was for his clarifying the arguments about the aircraft so concisely and factually. This method is known as comparison and contrast.

In a speech to a community group on world affairs at the end of the year, a speaker closed an eloquent talk with a prayer, which was most appropriate as he had been discussing trouble spots in the world. He had saved the prayer from a newspaper clipping that appeared following the flight of Apollo 8. It is the first prayer from space and was read to the world from Apollo 8. Everyone wanted a copy and wanted to know where it was from and who wrote it. So a prayer can be an effective type of content in any part of a speech. Here is the prayer:

"Give us, O God, the vision which can see thy love in the world in spite of human failure. Give us the faith to trust thy goodness in spite of our ignorance and weakness. Give us the knowledge to pray with understanding hearts, and show us what each one of us can do to set forward the coming of the day of universal peace. Amen."

Truly, stories, facts, information, illustrations, and statistics, even poems and prayers, are all around us. This is the material winning speeches are made from. Start watching, listening, and collecting some gems today. You'll find that your speechmaking will improve a hundredfold and that creating the speech will become easier and easier. Certainly, this is a large part of the success, for example, of Dr. Norman Vincent Peale. He is an outstanding preacher from the pulpit and also sought after as a speaker for community groups, service clubs, conventions, and sales rallies.

Dr. Peale fills his talks and sermons with stories of real people and real experiences. Often I've heard him begin with an incident such as, "I met a young man on an airplane flight recently from Denver to New York. He was sitting in the seat beside me. I was surprised to discover he was an expert on pyramids. He told me about the story of Napoleon once visiting the great pyramid of Giza. It was determined by Napoleon that if all the stones used to build the pyramid were stacked in a wall 10 feet high and 1 foot thick, the wall of stones from that one pyramid would extend all around France." Having hooked the audience with a brief opening incident that actually occurred, he then continued to make a point about creativity. He always fills the time allowed with inspiring, entertaining stories and is a prime example of a speaker vitally alive with optimism and enthusiasm.

While we are speaking of sermons and the Bible, a thought or two about the use of biblical quotations from the Old or the New Testament might be helpful here. Billy Graham often preaches with a Bible in his hand or on the lectern in front of him. Naturally, he quotes from it regularly. When President Carter took the oath of office in January 1977, his hand rested upon the Bible, which was opened to a text from Micah, one of the minor prophets of the Old Testament. The text is Verse 8, Chapter 6: "He hath shewed thee, O man, what is good; and what doth the Lord require of thee, but to do justly, and to love mercy, and to walk humbly with thy God?" When President Carter's predecessor, Gerald Ford, took his oath of office in August 1974, in the White House, he chose a text from Proverbs: Chapter 3, Verses 5 and 6: "Trust in the Lord with all thy heart; and lean not unto thine own understanding. In all the ways acknowledge Him, and He shall direct thy paths."

I suggest that you save clippings from newspapers and magazines of events such as the swearing-in of a president and that you note such texts or prayers used. Often you can highlight a speech or a sermon with just such examples. Note also that all the clippings you save could provide excellent material for writing articles or stories as well.

CHAPTER 3

Master Keys for Organizing Your Talk Professionally

ORGANIZATION STYLES OF THE PROFESSIONALS

Once you've collected all the data, statistics, examples, and illustrations you'll need for your presentation, you should apply the next rule: arrangement. So far you've identified your audience, limited your subject to one dominant idea or purpose, and gathered specific material suited to that purpose. Now you're ready to arrange the material in a definite order. The order or arrangement depends upon the material, the dominant purpose, and the particular audience.

Many professionals prefer to use sequential order, in which events are presented in sequence, such as a witness in the courtroom explaining exactly what happened leading up to an accident. Others choose to use chronological order, such as presenting the history of one's company, or the story of one's life. Another logical order is to use the past, present, future sequence. Just about any subject you could name would fit into this type of arrangement. For instance, suppose the topic of your speech is transportation. The past years could be highlighted by talking about the use of the horse and buggy, the present by talking about high-powered luxury cars, and the future by talking about the possible use of monorails as the principal means of moving people and materials.

You could also follow the order of analysis. Analysis, or identification of the real problem should provide answers to the following questions: what, when, who, where, and perhaps how, why, how many, how much, and how often? The answers to these questions are related. The analysis should include a statement of the objectives as they relate to the topic or the problem.

You may want to follow the order of importance. Begin with items that headline your idea and end with points that deserve highlighting, which could be the opening point restated or paraphrased.

Another type of organization is comparison and contrast. The speaker demonstrates to the audience the differences or similarities of an idea in order to get them to evaluate alternative methods or plans. A comparison could be as simple as something that I heard on a newscast over network radio recently. The commentator declared, "A baby born in New York City has a greater chance of being murdered than a serviceman who served in World War II!" Benjamin Franklin referred to this type or organization as the "Weighing Method." You can list the assets and the liabilities of an action or decision and compare the lists. It should be easier for an audience to make a decision if they are allowed to compare and contrast the gains or losses of an action.

A pattern or order used in technical presentations is the problem solving formula. Key questions such as these are asked: "What is the problem?" "What are the causes of the problem?" "What is needed?" "What is the best solution?" "Who will implement it?" "When will it be done?" This method is applicable to any talk in which the speaker wants to show what the situation is, what it should be, and what needs to be done. This pattern helps the audience to make a decision.

You can also combine two or more of these types of organization or arrangement. As a speaker, your task is to develop the best combination of material in terms of topic, audience, and objectives. For many longer talks you will need more than one style of arrangement. Often the type of talk you plan will suggest the style to use. The common kinds of talks are those that inform, entertain, convince (perhaps to change an attitude), impress, and persuade (to take action).

If you make a skeleton outline, it will force you to determine the order in which you're going to present your ideas. Instead of using the abstract words "introduction," "body," and "close," in your skeleton outline, which don't help at all, you could substitute for "introduction," the words "take hold," for "body" the word "transmit," and for "close" the words "drive home."

Start with a word picture, a story, or an image so that you'll have an entrance into the minds of the audience. Don't use just any incident or story but rather one that suits the particular dominant purpose and "takes hold" of the attention of the listeners. After "transmitting" your idea and the specific incidents, illustrations, or other evidence to support your point, you're ready to "drive home" your idea with an effective closing.

Those three concrete terms will form your skeleton outline, which will help you organize your talk. By using the outline you will force yourself to be specific rather than vague.

So far we've considered only ideas not words. But words are vital, since it is through words that we transmit our ideas clearly to others. Words are so important that I urge you to write and revise your content and above all be specific. Prefer the concrete, specific words to the general and abstract words. For instance, commonly used words such as "they say" are not specific enough. Here are three clearer expressions: "My neighbors, the Martins, say"; "Supervisor Jim Smith says"; "My friend Jack Jones says." Providing specific names, numbers, and places contributes to clarity, understanding, and action. Just as one drop of ink in a glass of water changes the color of the water, so one word can change the meaning of an idea. You will understand this idea of specificity more clearly if I give you an illustration:

> A supervisor told a new postal employee in New York City in his first week on the job to, "Take the truck and deliver the mail." Hours later the supervisor got a phone call from the new employee, who said, "I'm out of gas on the New Jersey Turnpike 20 miles out of New York. Can you send me help so I can deliver this load of mail?" The supervisor had forgotten to be specific. Delivering the mail meant driving it down the street to Pennsylvania Station and leaving it on the loading platform.

In review, I've suggested that you *limit* your topic to one dominant purpose; *select* specific material suited solely to that purpose; and *arrange* the specific material in a definite order and outline. Now I've added the suggestion that you *write and revise* the material, selecting the most suitable words. And I suggest that you write the key ideas only. It's preferable to list the key ideas in sequence rather than word-for-word. Paper always comes between you and the audience. As Bishop Fulton J. Sheen once observed in a television talk on speeches, "Never submit an active mind to a dead sheet of paper."

Using your skeleton outline you can build your talk from your notes rather than by writing everything out word for word. I would suggest that you use no more than three or four main headings and that you use key words for your subheadings as reminders of your supporting material.

HOW TO ESTABLISH A RAPPORT RAPIDLY

Let's get specific now and talk about the actual content of your speech, starting with your opening words, usually in answer to an introduction. What you say as you begin will either gain a rapport with the audience or fail to do so. You have an excellent chance for rapport if you respond to the toastmaster or toastmistress, the person who will introduce you to the audience.

A "thank you" is always the first requirement when someone presents you, and that's all that is necessary. However, professionals often use this as an opportunity to win a rapport or condition the audience to themselves and their presentation. I heard one speaker react to a long reading of his years of accomplishments with these words, "bewitching inaccuracies of biography." The audience laughed at the response, and the speaker won a rapport with that opening thought. The speaker had revealed herself, and what she revealed was a sense of humor and humility. Another speaker who was confronted with the same kind of flattering introduction responded in this way: "Now I know how it feels to be a waffle smothered in syrup." That thought evoked a laugh from the audience and gained their attention and interest.

The objective of the first words you speak should be to inspire the audience to want to listen to you. There is no end to the possibilities of responding to the introduction. A clever response is just one suggestion. Anything that you say to identify a common bond between you or your topic and the audience will work wonders in establishing a rapport. For example, talk about something topical, or something in common with the audience, or possibly give them a human insight into family, sports, pets, or even the funny papers.

Former President Gerald Ford, in his first press conference in 1974, began with a true anecdote about his wife. She had scheduled her first press conference for the same day, but she postponed hers for a week on the condition that the President would prepare his own meals while she prepared for her press conference. The anecdote won an instant rapport with the Press Corps.

Another example of a good opening is the following story. A consultant from Pennsylvania, who was to speak on Management by Objectives, was introduced to an audience of 100 executives. It was the morning after Billie Jean King devastated Bobby Riggs in their historic tennis match on TV. The speaker thanked the individual for the introduction, paused, and then, looking out at the audience said, "Tennis anyone?" The executives laughed heartily and then applauded. A strong rapport was achieved with two clever, topical words.

Of course it is not always necessary to say anything, planned or spontaneous, before you begin with your actual prepared opening, but don't overlook the opportunity for making your audience want to listen to you, before you begin.

OPENINGS THAT CAPTURE AND HOLD ATTENTION

An arresting opening has one or more of these four characteristics:

It arouses interest.
It orients the audience to what will be covered.
It directs the attention of the audience to your chief purpose or idea.
It reveals yourself.

Here are some examples that fulfill one or more of these four qualities. Earlier I suggested that you use the best method of all to open your speech: present an incident, or a mental picture. Stories, parables, or anecdotes not only capture the mind but also are memorable. Again, I suggest you begin your talk with a slice-of-life incident.

I recall a true-life example in a talk I heard some years ago. The speaker began, "I'll never forget the day 17 years ago when I was 16 years old. The judge looked down at me in the court and said, 'You're sentenced to prison for the rest of your natural life'." Of course, the speaker already had 100 percent of the audience's attention. This speaker went on to explain that he was an ex-convict who decided to lead a model prison life. He had been paroled earlier that year after serving 17 years of a life sentence. Any story, projected with feeling, gains immediate attention.

Another technique popular with professional speakers is to ask for a show of hands, rather than to open with a rhetorical question. A show of hands involves the audience, whereas a rhetorical question does not. A sales trainer often opens his presentation by using the show-of-hands method and wins immediate attention as well as a rapport. After acknowledging the chair, this speaker says, "I'd like to take a little market survey. And I'd like a show of hands on this. How many of you have heard me before? How many haven't heard me before? How many don't care either way?" For a well-known speaker, this brings an instant laugh and a rapport with the audience.

A rhetorical question is one you don't want the audience to answer. An example would be, "If you were the president of the United States for one day, what is the first thing you would change?" This type of question is more effective if it is placed in the body of the talk rather than in the beginning. It is excellent as a transition and provides a good change of pace. Questions are always attention-getters because they let members of the audience share, at least mentally.

Although I'll be discussing the importance of visual aids in the next chapter, I want to emphasize now the value of visual aids to open your speech. It's a natural technique for gaining the interest of your listeners. You might hold up an object, have something written on a flip-chart or chalkboard that you reveal in your opening, or show a picture or a poster. The more relevant the visual aid is to your topic, the better it aids you in gaining the attention and interest of the audience.

One of the best openings I ever heard was provided by a speech teacher from London appearing on the old Groucho Marx television program, "You Bet Your Life." This speaker was illustrating how to win the interest of the audience immediately. His method is known as *arousing suspense*. Holding out a clenched fist, this speaker said, "I have something in my hand that no human being has ever seen before, and a moment after I open my hand, no one will ever see it again," After a long pause the speaker opened his hand and revealed a peanut in a shell. He broke open the shell, picked up the peanut, and ate it. He made his point without saying another word, and he had gained instantly the audience's attention. In the sentence, "No one had ever seen it before, no one will ever see it again" there was suspense, a visual aid, and a startling fact—all in the same opening.

Your opening story should support your idea or subject, otherwise don't use it. This should be your guiding principle. Don't use stories or illustrations that have nothing to do with the points you're trying to get across.

Another type of opening that pulls in an audience is the statement of an arresting fact. I was present in the audience and heard this one. A famous heart specialist was speaking, and he opened with this statement: "Four out of five men in this audience will die of heart disease." He captured our attention completely and went on to explain why the statement was true, but more important, what each of us could do to prevent the prediction from coming true. Again, the fact must support the main idea or point of your talk, or reject it. And always be certain it is a true statement, statistic, or fact. Accuracy is essential for speakers.

A final suggestion is warranted here on "take hold" types of openings. Many speakers have excellent success with the *promise opener*: you promise the audience something genuine. It could be a promise to help them save time, money, mistakes, or a problem. People naturally want to know how you and your talk will benefit them. This is really just basic selling. In advertising it's known as the "USP", *unique selling proposition*. The idea is to offer the consumer a specific benefit, unique to the product advertised. For example, for years consumers have heard in radio and TV commercials that, "Wonder Bread builds strong bodies 12 ways" or that Anacin's combination of ingredients gives "fast . . . fast . . . fast relief" and that Colgate "cleans your breath while it cleans your teeth."

People want to know how to improve their lives, health, success, skills, and abilities. In a speech contest of banking people, which I judged, the woman who won opened by saying, "I'm going to tell you how to get rich!" She went on to prove how through savings anyone could have a large estate by retirement age. With the Keogh Savings Plan for self-employed people it's possible for an individual to accrue nearly $500,000 by age 70 through saving $7500 a year in the plan, starting at age 25.

But the time arrives—and early in your talk—when you must state your case and orient the audience to the exact point of your message. Some openings accomplish this as an inherent part of the incident or anecdote used to capture attention. Other openings stimulate interest but the point still needs to be stated in order to tie-in the story with the dominant idea of the talk.

For example, earlier in this chapter the "peanut opener" was given as an example of an amusing and suspenseful opener, but this still needed to be tied to the rest of the speech. The speaker went on to say, "And your ideas are of no more value than this peanut in its shell unless you express them." He added, "This course will help you develop that ability." Now he had the audience's attention and they knew the point of his speech, all in the first minute. It's important to state clearly the point of your talk in the first minute or two (usually, the sooner the better).

To summarize how to open a speech or a presentation, the audience should feel your desire to put your ideas across to them. You can do this by revealing your point or purpose in an emphatic way, and you should let your listeners know your attitude, your conviction, and the reason for your position.

ARRANGING ILLUSTRATIONS, EVIDENCE, STORIES, AND SUPPORTING DATA

We're now ready to follow our arresting opening with illuminating illustrations or solid evidence. The first knowledge you need is an awareness of types of examples. The acronym SEDATE will help you recall them quickly: Statistics, Exhibit, Demonstration, Analogy, Testimony (of an expert), and Experience. Concrete data or evidence revolves around these key types of examples.

It is necessary to build support for your main point or points. The only effective way of doing this is through the use of specifics, not generalities. One way of doing this is by providing quotes that serve as testimony. For example, if you are talking about a scar you have on your hand, *you* are the expert giving the testimony.

Current, provable statistics are another solid form of evidence. Again, an analogy or comparison is generally the most effective way to convey dry statistics and prove your point.

For example, stating that there are 17,000 restaurants in New York City isn't as graphic as saying that you can eat in a different restaurant in New York City every morning, noon, and night for 15 years and still you would not have eaten in all the restaurants in the city.

If you plan to use an exhibit or visual aid for support and evidence, there are many methods available to you. Statistics in visual form, or any fact or idea supported by visual aids will help you make your point more clearly and convincingly. I believe it's true that one picture is worth 10,000 words. So save your words and make your point accurately with graphs, charts, objects, slides, or a model.

An experience out of your life would be an incident you've lived through—something you personally witnessed, heard, or read about. It could be a business experience or relate to a hobby, sport, or interest you have, or your education or family. Nothing compares with personal experience for capturing and holding an audience's attention and for convincing and persuading the audience to believe or do what you want them to do.

You are the most important visual aid in any speech you present, so don't overlook demonstrating something for your listeners. Don't just talk about how to do an activity or operate a piece of equipment; demonstrate it. Use the real object if possible or simulate the object to show how to use it.

Dr. Ralph Nichols, from the University of Minnesota, demonstrates the power of the ear in his talks on listening. He asks the members of the audience to close their eyes. Then he talks from different parts of the stage. He asks various members from the audience to point to where they think he's standing as he talks, and by doing this he proves that the ear is quicker than the eye. He illustrates that the ear alone, without sight, can guide someone to wherever he moves or to wherever he's standing as he talks.

Almost every idea, concrete or abstract, can be demonstrated or illustrated. Brainstorm for ways to illustrate your speeches and make them exciting show-and-tell experiences for your listeners.

I have said enough about the methods and techniques for building support in the middle of your speech. Now I will give you some criteria for supporting your evidence. Your factual data should be relevant, accurate, easy to explain, clear, and effective against counterarguments. Always be able to corroborate your claims and identify the source of your facts and statistics. If you are unable to substantiate your statements, then your credibility with the audience will be jeopardized.

STYLES OF EFFECTIVE TRANSITIONS AND BRIDGES

The next step in arranging your examples and evidence is to find simple, short transitions that will help you achieve a smooth flow in your speech. Some examples of transitional words are: also, another, however, next, so far, again, in summary, and to review.

Try to keep a thread going through your talk to tie it all together and command continuing interest from the audience. You can ensure the interest of your listeners and their understanding of your ideas if you use oral road signs such as, "The point I want to make is . . . ," or "In this talk I want to identify three characteristics of a professional." It's trite to say, "I want to make one thing perfectly clear," but it is important nevertheless to be explicit in telling the audience your key points. For example, you might say, "The one idea I want to explain is this."

The use of rhetorical questions is an excellent form of transition and can serve as attention-getters when they are sprinkled throughout a speech. If you were giving a talk on management expertise and you pointed out a problem situation, you could ask a rhetorical question, a question you wanted the listeners to think about and not answer audibly. Their mental answers will help keep them involved in your speech.

For a clearer understanding of our ideas, the audience needs warning signs and signals in a speech. These are known as *transitions*, or *bridges*. You should use them to move from one idea to another or from one supporting point to another. Some unique types of transitions include pausing (short, long, or very long), moving from one side of the platform to the other, giving a mini-summary, refocusing on a main point, or even asking for a show of hands during the speech.

A transition can also serve as a change of pace. I heard a master speechmaker use the following as a transition. He had been talking for 15 minutes in an after-dinner speech to 2,000 men and women. He suddenly stopped and asked, "Can you hear me alright in back?" They answered, "Yes!" And the speaker then said, "Well, you haven't missed anything yet anyway." With that the audience laughed heartily, and the speaker had their full attention as he continued.

I once heard a speaker who, after 45 minutes of a one-hour address, stopped and asked the audience, "Have I been on too long?" Of course they replied, "No!" Then the speaker said, "Well, I'd rather you would say I've been on too long than to hear you say later, 'He had three chances to quit.' " He got a laugh, applause, and renewed interest from his listeners.

You should try to avoid tired, worn, or dull cliches. For instance, instead of saying, "There's something new under the sun," which is trite, you could say, "There's something new under Telstar," because that satellite is spinning around our globe constantly. *Reader's Digest* offers in each issue a full-page of picturesque speech and patter. A little time spent in thinking of an original way to express an idea will provide fresh, catchy, and memorable phrases. Innovation is badly needed in speechmaking. I've always loved some of Mae West's original lines, such as, "Too much of a good thing is wonderful."

EIGHT PROFESSIONAL CLOSINGS

Most professors and professional speechmakers consider the closing of a speech to be the most important part of the speech. Perhaps this is so because it is the final thought. Also, many surveys and tests reveal that people remember best what is said in the closing of speeches. Even if your listeners have been dozing or daydreaming, you have a chance in your closing sentences to make your key point or points clearly, concisely, and convincingly. There are only about eight classic closings the top professionals use to end their speeches, but there are endless possibilities for innovation in closing a speech. A list of the best methods for closing a speech effectively would include:

1. a summary of your key ideas
2. a restatement of your main point
3. a call to action
4. a poem
5. a quotation
6. a moral to your story
7. an anecdote
8. a visual aid.

It might be best to think of a humorous type of closing as an anecdote. You could use either a personal experience or an amusing incident you read or heard. Remember, however, that if you are poking fun at someone, it's always wiser and safer to poke fun at yourself, not the audience. One speaker told a joke in closing but no one laughed, so she ad-libbed, "Now I know what to do when you lay an egg before an audience. Just step back and admire it." She stepped back two steps, looked down at the floor, and at that point got a loud response of generous laughter from the audience, which saved the speech and the day for her. Now, let's review the more professional and popular types of closings with specific illustrations.

There's innovation in the closing of a talk I heard a speaker give recently. He closed with a unique poem that won him a standing ovation. It should be noted that he kept his talk short. Here's the poem he used to end his speech: "I love a finished speaker, yes indeed I do! I don't mean one who's polished, I just mean one who's through!" Then he shouted, "I'm through!" and sat down to ringing applause.

Of course, you could also close a serious talk with a poem. One speech I heard was entitled, "Stop Feeling Sorry for Yourself." The speaker closed by saying, "So Count Your Blessings! And to help you stop feeling sorry for yourself, remember this poem: 'I had the blues because I had no shoes, until upon the street, I met a man who had no feet!' "

I use a quotation to close presentations when I have involved the audience members in participation exercises. I tell them that a Ralph Waldo Emerson statement applies to me working with them, and to them helping one another. Here's the quotation: "Every person I meet is in some way my superior, it's that I try to learn from him or her." And to reinforce a talk you might give on being a better listener, you can close by quoting from the Bible, St. Mark reporting Christ's words: "If any man has ears to hear, let him listen. And unto those who hear shall more be given."

Keep in mind that the closing of your talk is probably what the audience will remember longest. As you prepare a brief, to-the-point closing, do it with words that help show the intensity and strength of feeling that this vital portion of your speech requires. In fact, remind yourself that you're not putting a tack in the wall but you're driving a stake into the ground as you emphasize or reemphasize your one dominant purpose or idea.

In a speech in which you are asking the audience to do something, the request should be something possible and easy to accomplish. For example, in recent years the Red Cross increased the intensity of their appeal for blood donors. One volunteer I heard gave a stirring talk, just about five minutes in length. In the closing she said, "Here's what I'm urging each one of you to do: Give a pint of blood!" At this point she got down on her knees and added, "I beg you to help others. Please raise your hand if you'll give a pint of blood in the next two weeks through the Red Cross. Please stand if you have your hand up." And in those few moments she had everyone standing in testimony to their willingness to donate a pint of blood within two weeks. The speaker said, "Thank you for giving the gift of life to others." This type of closing is a call to action.

The best example I've ever heard for closing a talk with an anecdote was demonstrated in a sermon by a foreign missionary. He gave a brief introduction of himself and the African missions he had served. He added that the missions' needs included prayers, food, and money, which took only two minutes. Then he closed with this anecdote.

> "Irishman Mike was 75 years old. Neighbors learned that he had inherited $100,000 from a distant relative in Ireland. His friends feared that he would suffer a heart attack because of heart trouble when he heard the startling news, so they called in Father Murphy, his parish pastor, to break it to him gently.
>
> "Father Murphy said, 'Mike, let's do some supposing. Let's suppose that somebody in your family left you a gift in their will of $100,000. What would you do with it?' 'Ah, shucks, Father Murphy,' Mike replied, 'there's no one left in my family, and anyway, no one that I can recall ever had that kind of money.' 'But,' persisted Father Murphy, 'just suppose you did inherit $100,000. What would you do with it?' Mike snapped back, 'Golly, Father, I'd give it all to you for the church!' and the priest died of a heart attack."

I was an usher in the church the Sunday morning the missionary told that story. I never saw so much money put in the collection baskets following such a brief sermon and humorous closing (three minutes total). Parishioners pulled out $5, $10, and $20 bills and loaded the collection baskets. The missionary never directly appealed for money; the closing anecdote accomplished that for him superbly.

The great writer Aesop was outstanding for his short-story telling, yet his stories always had a moral to them. We've all heard about the goose that laid the golden eggs. The owner was greedy and killed the goose to get more gold, but there was none. The moral of Aesop's story was "Don't get greedy or you can lose everything." And it's worth noting that most of Aesop's fables are short stories, yet make memorable points through the use of illustration.

Probably the most popular type of closing for speeches is a summary of your main points, or if you're making just one point, a paraphrasing of that idea. For instance, if you're giving a speech on the necessity for registering and voting as a responsibility of citizenship and as a safeguard to freedom, you might make that clear early in your presentation. Then, in closing you could state the point in a different way by paraphrasing the key idea. In this case to close you might say, "Freedom is a two-sided coin. One side is freedom, and the other side is responsibility. To protect our freedom, it is the duty and responsibility of every eligible American to register and vote. I urge *you* to vote and to get others to do so."

Perhaps the most popular closing of professional speakers is a summary of the main points. This is most effective because it leaves fresh in the minds of the audience precisely what you had in mind and wanted to get across to them. Also, it condenses your essential ideas. Remember, the summary should be brief (the shorter the better), as long as the main ideas are covered. An example follows.

If you were giving a speech on the characteristics of a dynamic sales representative and you had made three points in a speech of 15 or 20 minutes, the closing could be short and simple. You could summarize it by quoting the words of a sales trainer closing a training session for insurance sales representatives: "In review, the three traits that have helped me get to the $1 million round table are the same characteristics that I look for in sales representatives: one, a deep interest in people; two, enthusiasm; three, persistence. And the most important of these three is a deep interest in people."

A review or summary could also include a brief illustration to highlight the main point, but it should reinforce your idea.

Here is one warning, however. The worst way to close a speech is to offer a plain and aimless "Thank You!" This takes away from an effective closing. It's important to show gratitude, but it should be genuine and specific, for example, "Thank you for your response" or "for your participation." Always mention what you're thanking the audience for, unless it's obvious.

A final suggestion for closing a presentation is that you can use a visual aid to make the point for you. One speaker I heard closed with a spicy story and turned an overhead projector on to reveal the closing thought on the screen. It read: "Rated X!" The speaker is an older man, and the cute but inoffensive anecdote made the visual finale even funnier.

Earlier I suggested that you think of the words "drive home" rather than "closing" when you are outlining your speech. I also mentioned earlier that it is necessary to prepare lively words for a closing that will help you drive a stake, not just put a tack in the wall. The idea is to present your key points with intensity. The closing of your speech should be a highlight, a high point. Recall Patrick Henry's words to the Virginia Convention in March, 1775, in closing a stirring and eloquent speech, "Is life so dear, or peace so sweet, as to be purchased at the price of chains and slavery? Forbid it, Almighty God! I know not what course others may take, But as for me, give me liberty, or give me death!"

CHAPTER 4

Professional Methods for Using Visual Aids

PERFECTING THE PRIMARY VISUAL AID: YOURSELF

A few years ago Marshall McLuhan, a professor at Toronto University, stirred a world-wide response with his statement, "The medium is the message." He once defined that remark by saying, "The medium is the 'massage' of the eyes." He further suggested that when you or I are talking to one or more persons, we are the message, not the content of our speaking; that is, our behavior, example, facial expressions, posture, and tone of voice, become the message communicated.

This declaration that the speaker is the message is the very reason I say that the primary visual aid when you are speaking is yourself. Senator Hayakawa of California, a former semantics professor, states it this way: "In this age of television, image is more important than substance." When ABC paid Barbara Walters $5 million to join their TV network as a news commentator and interviewer, they were supplying the proof for McLuhan's statement.

Television has made people more aware and more accustomed to visuals of all kinds. But my point is that all kinds of visuals will avail the speaker little if the image, the personality, appearance, vitality, posture, and voice aren't projecting an honest, sincere, and natural person. So be sure you are at your best when you are delivering a speech. E. E. Cummings noted, "To be nobody-but-yourself in a world which is doing its best, night and day, to make you everybody else, means to fight the hardest battle which any human being can fight—and never stop fighting." Don't try to be anyone but yourself at your confident best. Be alive. Think alive. Act alive. Talk alive. If the audience is bored, restless, and falling asleep, it's the speaker's fault. Get excited and keep them awake.

BENEFITS OF USING VISUAL AIDS

Since youngsters entering the first grade have seen 5,000 hours of TV on the average and high school graduates have seen 15,000 hours of TV, a speaker who isn't alive vocally and visually will not command attention from the audience. This is also the first of two reasons that visual aids are expected and necessary for effective speaking today. Even professional speakers seek some sort of visual aids for large audiences of thousands. The usual visual aids such as flip charts, chalkboards, posters, or slides couldn't be seen by an audience of 500 or more, but some other type of visual aid is often used.

For example, Ira Hayes, spokesman for National Cash Register Corp., uses such props as a Davy Crockett hat, real money, toys, cards, and even cereal boxes. One of the best visual aids is a real object. Hayes says that he uses props because "People can't watch a radio; they get restless."

A second reason that visual aids are expected and necessary is that 85 percent of everything we learn in life comes through our eyes. Only about 11 percent of what the mind retains comes through our ears. These figures are the strongest argument for visual aids, because they show that a speaker or lecturer who doesn't use visual aids is at a disadvantage when compared to one who does.

Further, the American Management Association, which has been training people in management throughout the world since 1923, says that they've found through testing that there is only a 10 percent return on an average lecture, but this percentage jumps to as high as 50 percent when a presentation has been made with visual aids. And this percentage hits 70 percent when there are visual aids and audience participation as well.

So, in a nutshell, visuals aids of any kind will increase audience interest. Also, technical or complex concepts, statistics, and ideas can be simplified with charts, slides, maps, or illustrations. Visual aids not only increase retention but also make it easy to relate the different aspects of a subject. Visual aids convey correct impressions and eliminate the misunderstanding that comes from words alone. That's why the Oriental saying, "One time seeing is worth a thousand times hearing" is so apt now.

KEY QUALITIES OF AN EFFECTIVE VISUAL AID

Visual aids are used to support presentations of any kind. This means designing each visual aid to perform a specific function, but remember that a visual aid is just that—an aid—not a crutch or a substitute. Use them to highlight key ideas or to clarify and to simplify technical or financial data. Don't worry about using too many. Just be sure you are using visual aids where they are needed and not just for the sake of having visual aids in your speech. They should always relate to the subject. A poor or an inappropriate visual aid will detract from the speech.

A good visual aid should be simple, legible, and appropriate, and they should be planned carefully. They should be colorful in design, realistic, and easily manageable. Above all, data used in visual aids and in your speech must be accurate. Misrepresentation and dishonesty are the biggest blocks to communication.

DO'S AND DON'T'S OF USING VISUAL AIDS

Use visual aids to show what something looks like. Use the real object or article if possible or obtain a picture of it. Pie charts can be useful for breaking down complex concepts and for adding interest and clarity. For example, you can use a pie chart, as magazines and newspapers do, to show where our tax dollars go: one portion to government, one portion to defense, welfare, and so on.

Printed visual aids should be large, clear, legible, and brief. Don't try to say everything in one visual aid. You have a choice of slides, transparencies, flannel boards, chalkboards. videotapes, films, charts, objects, pictures, and even tape recorders to help you.

Overhead projectors (for transparencies) and 35MM-slide projectors are the most commonly used visual aids in classrooms, adult education, and sales training programs. One problem with slide projectors, however, is that the lights have to be turned out or down, whereas with overhead projectors or filmstrips, the lights can be left on. Lights that are turned out too long during a presentation tend to turn people off; they become tired, sluggish, lazy, and this makes it difficult to continue holding their interest. With rear-screen projection the problem with slide projectors is overcome.

Use only large, capital letters, always printed, on chalkboards, flipcharts, slides, and posters. All visual aids, with the exception of photographs or slides, should always be titled and numbered. You could use letters as well as numbers (either arabic letters or roman numerals) to make it easier for the audience to follow specific points. Using asterisks or stars to highlight points would also be appropriate.

Make drawings large and use heavy lines. Try to use a variety of colors to add interest and contrast. People respond to color. Remember, most members of your audience will be accustomed to color TV and technicolor films. Use darker colors, which show more richly and clearly: red, black, blue, or green. Keep away from orange, brown, and other lighter shades, because it's harder to see them. You can use red for loss and green for profit, for example, in a chart showing the financial status of a company or organization. Or you can use color in a graph to show the comparison of growth or decrease in sales over a period of months or years. Look through newsmagazines, such as *U.S. News and World Report* and *Newsweek*, to see how their graphics illustrate trends, statistics, and comparisons. You'll find many ideas for visual aids also from newspapers and TV news programs.

Every speaker should learn to make his or her own visual aids on a flip chart or a chalkboard. Usually, flip-chart material should be prepared in advance.

Always test your visual aids ahead of time by trying them out on someone. If possible, test them in the room or auditorium where you'll actually be speaking. Set them up and then go to the sides and the back of the room to see if they can be read easily or if any pictures can be seen clearly. Redo them if they can't be read, seen, or understood easily.

Avoid talking toward your visual aid. Face the audience always, glance at the visual, but talk toward the audience. Remember, with or without visual aids, the unforgivable fault is to neglect to look at your audience as much of the time as possible, if not all the time. The visual aids can't speak, so you are still the key communicator. And never stand in front of what you are showing.

Avoid too much detail, illegible or crowded writing or printing, too small a visual aid, or wrong emphasis. Hold the visual aids up so all can see them. Don't rush anything you display. Give everyone time to see and understand what you've chosen to highlight in your speech.

You should keep all visual aids out of sight until you are ready to show them, and put them aside when you've finished using them. Keep all visual aids from blocking your face if you are holding them up for the audience to see. And remember that practice makes perfect when you are designing and using visual aids. Experience will teach you correct placement, how many to use, the appropriate sequence, and smooth handling of visual aids.

EXHIBITING AND DEMONSTRATING EVIDENCE

By *evidence* I mean all of your facts, statistics, quotations, or other supporting data that you choose to project in visual aids. Few cases in court are won without tangible evidence. If you've ever served on a jury you know that evidence plays a major role in influencing the jury's decision. I've seen large chalkboards, huge maps, giant graphs, slides, blown-up photographs, real objects, and charts used in court cases. Attorneys have been known to add a great deal of what is so badly needed today in public presentations: originality, drama, and innovation. Being original, dramatic, or innovative takes some time and planning, but creativity will result and you'll be more successful in your presentations. Of course, I've also seen all of these types of visual aids used in classrooms, conventions, and just about everywhere presentations are made or teaching takes place.

There are several types of charts and a variety of uses for them in presenting evidence or essential data. In most cases the charts would be prepared ahead of time. Still, there are many times when you'll want to fill in portions of a chart as you speak or record ideas from the audience as they are given. In such instances it helps if you have an assistant to record the responses—it's more professional and it saves time. A flip chart is the basic visual tool of speakers, teachers, and even salespeople today. It is versatile. The portable type on an easel is much easier and neater to work with than a chalkboard. It is also flexible and has many uses. Besides being used to give emphasis and to make ideas clearer, the flip chart can be used to record decisions, ideas, agreements, or other data contributed by audience members.

Getting the audience involved is a key to a successful speech. Psychologists tell us that "People don't care unless they share." Giving listeners a chance to contribute and writing their responses down on a chart provides the best kind of participation. Actually, individuals in a classroom or members of an audience often learn more from fellow participants than they do from a speaker. So find ways to involve the audience in your talk. It's also true that individuals learn more when they are teachers than when they are just listeners. We learn from each other, when given the chance, and we learn by doing.

One long-standing rule of communication has been to cover just one point or one idea at a time. A point-by-point chart, or a cellophane overlay chart are perfect for this technique. In a point-by-point chart, each line or idea is covered by a strip of paper taped on one end with scotch tape. The speaker pulls off the strips one at a time to reveal each point separately.

The overlay chart is a series of points illustrated on a transparency cut into sections and attached by tape to a full-size visual aid. This technique is used to show how something works—a process or an operation. I usually find that one with six sections (overlay pieces) would probably be the maximum necessary. Often, just one overlay is enough and adds interest, clarity, and variety to a presentation. These ideas of point-by-point charts and overlays can be accomplished on an overhead projector or on a flip chart. Again, the easiest way to simplify technical or financial data is by using visual aids. Always try to put statistics into the form of analogy or comparison so your listeners will understand them. Salespeople know the value of breaking down costs to the lowest figures. Someone selling an insurance policy for a college education for your child could have you figure out the cost per day on a pocket calculator. This provides participation for you, and you see the final figures lit up on the calculator. It might turn out to be just $1.96 a day for the policy, and you probably gave more than that in a tip for the last meal that you ate in a restaurant. Isn't that small sum easier to buy than a $10,000 policy at $715.00 a year? In actuality, it might not be any easier, but salespeople know that it appears that way to others.

When you are showing technical or financial charts, graphs, or diagrams, use a pointer. Whether you are tall or short, the pointer will make it easier for you to describe the content of your visual aid and will make it easier for the audience to follow the explanation or interpretation. However, don't keep the pointer in your hand when you aren't using it and don't play with it or point it at the audience. By following these tips you'll get your message across clearly without distracting your listeners.

HOW TO PICK THE RIGHT KIND OF VISUAL AID

In selecting a visual aid list your key ideas and then ask yourself: "How will a visual aid help?" "What visual aid will work best?" If you give yourself plenty of time to think about it, your imagination will go to work for you and bring ideas to mind. Of course, asking someone else can help you come up with ideas too. Originality is said to be a fresh pair of eyes.

Other questions to consider include, "What size room or auditorium will I be in?" "What size will the audience be?" "How will the audience be seated?" "Is there a high stage, or will I be speaking on the same level as the audience?" Sometimes stages are only 1 or 2 feet off ground level, but this will make it easier for the audience to see your visual aids. If you're on the same level as a large audience and you're short, it will be difficult to show charts or pictures. If the size of the audience is over 500 people, it is senseless to try and use a flip chart, a chalkboard, an overhead projector, or ordinary size charts or photographs. Therefore, the size of the audience will help you determine what can't be used. However, some small visual aids, such as the real object you're talking about can be used with any size audience. I try to show what I'm talking about even though many can't see it. I'll even take a 3 × 5 card out of my pocket or billfold and say, "I've written down my goals and the steps to achieve them and I keep the card right here in my pocket." The card then becomes evidence, concrete and visible enough even in the back of the auditorium. In fact, once I took out my wallet and a 3 × 5 card out of it before 2000 people. I showed them the bent and worn card that contained eight pep talks on it for quick reference and quick motivation anytime. I then read off two or three as samples. The people in the back could see I had something in my hand, and they heard me read from the list. It was a strong type of evidence, even though it was hard to see.

In the previous chapter I gave you an example of "the peanut opening" once used on a TV program. Even though the large audience couldn't see the peanut when the speaker opened his hand, when he said, "What I have in my hand is a peanut. I'm breaking it open and eating the peanut," the effect was the same as if they could see the peanut because the speaker made clear what was happening.

I'll often cut out quotations, statistics, and facts from current newspapers and magazines and either tape or type the information on 3 × 5 or 4 × 6 cards. I'll also add the source and date. Then, when I'm speaking, I simply take out the card, identify the source and date, and read the item. (Listeners today want to know the source of the material and the date as well.) By doing this you'll have all the information on one card. Also, you'll be able to quote exactly without having to paraphrase or memorize.

There's one professional speaker making the speaking circuit of conventions and banquets who gives humorous speeches. However, he himself says very little. He has a tape recorder and with it presents great storytellers, past as well as present telling their best jokes: Myron Cohen, Milton Berle, Dale Carnegie, Jack Benny, and Fred Allen. His audiences love it. Most of the jokes are timeless and get laughs today even though they are recorded. Innovation is paying off in a big way for this speaker.

A few words about handouts, a special type of visual aid. People like to take things away from speeches they hear. Ordinarily, don't distribute these handouts until the end of your talk. For larger groups you should have someone else distribute them. If it is necessary to give them out during your speech, never give more than one at a time and have the members of the audience read them along with you.

In summary, there are two key questions you should ask yourself

CHAPTER 5

Secrets for a Masterful Delivery

METHODS THE PROFESSIONALS USE TO REHEARSE

Name a successful speaker, actor, or preacher and the chances are that there's a story about how they practiced to develop their voice and speaking style. Going back in history, Demosthenes yearned to be an orator so he could influence others. He asked a famous actor, Satyrus, what to do. Satyrus told him he could only acquire the ability through practice. We've all heard how Demosthenes used pebbles from the ocean to improve his speech. I did the same thing in my teens in the Marine Corps during my free time. I gathered small pebbles from the ocean, washed them, and put them in my mouth. Then I recited such tongue twisters as, "Peter Piper picked a peck of pickled peppers." When I could say these tongue twisters clearly enough for someone to understand me through the pebbles, I knew that I was enunciating well enough to go on to other efforts.

Demosthenes used pebbles, but we are not told what he recited for practice. We do know that he retreated to a cave to practice in private. He had to work hard, we're told, because he was a stutterer with a poor, irritating voice. He even shaved his head to force himself to stay hidden so he would keep working hard to improve. Through persistent, long sessions he improved greatly. Then he began speaking in public and improved even more.

Winston Churchill and Abraham Lincoln were not born silver-tongued orators. They both studied other speakers, practiced endlessly, sought speaking engagements, and prepared meticulously. Both became great orators. And remember, Churchill also used pebbles to practice pronunciation and enunciation. You could also use M & M candies or marbles instead of pebbles.

Arthur Godfrey once confessed that he would sit down and talk to the pillars in his basement when he was a young man. Billy Graham said he practiced by talking to trees in the woods in his home state of North Carolina. Daniel Webster practiced speaking in empty auditoriums.

When wire recorders became available in the 1940s I used one to practice on. By the 1950s I had a tape recorder, and now just about every family has one, as they're inexpensive. It's an ideal way to practice because you can hear your improvement and also what you should keep working on: pitch, pace, emphasis, pauses, force, or variety.

One eighteenth-century Englishman, Charles James Fox, developed his speaking ability in a unique way. Fox gained his mastery of speech at the expense of Parliament. He made it a habit to jump up and say a few words on every matter that came before Parliament, regardless of how trivial the matter was. The matter may have been minor, but the experience Fox gained in effective speaking was not minor. He became one of England's most famous orators. He also knew when to quit, for he was known for his brevity.

But let's look at some modern methods of practice. Personally, like many other professional speakers, I prefer the method of practicing with a videotape recorder. I insist that corporations and organizations where I am teaching speaking have video equipment and a large monitor for playback, because it means my students can speak and then see and hear their speeches as they are played back for a critique of content and delivery. In this way nervous mannerisms, poor posture, serious facial expressions, and an overabundance of hand movements (or lack of them), can be corrected immediately. Also, voice problems can be corrected more easily once students hear themselves.

Find a university or an adult education speech course where videotape is used to help you polish your speaking. It's a powerful tool. Video equipment is rentable by the day or week in every large city, and there are portable units as well, so if you can't find a speech course this is an alternative you should consider.

Dr. Herb True, a former history professor at Notre Dame University, gives about 250 talks every year at conventions and banquets around the world. I rank him as one of the top five professional speakers in the United States. He records his speeches with a tape recorder and then, before he gives the speech again, he listens to the tape to learn how to improve it for the next occasion. If he is on an airplane or in a public place, he uses a pocket recorder and an earplug to listen to the tape.

Often, in conversation over dinner or elsewhere when Dr. True hears an interesting statement or fact, he'll ask the speaker to repeat it into the recorder. In this way he has the actual quotation directly from the person in his or her own voice. One day over lunch he had me repeat this phrase into his recorder, "People catch more than they learn"; that is, from peoples' actions or examples we learn more than from what they say. Or, in modern form, "The medium is the message."

Take heart from the experience of a clergyman I know from the Midwest who is one of the finest speakers in the country. He told me that he grew up as a confirmed stutterer, but he had always wanted to be able to inspire others through giving stirring and eloquent sermons. So he bought a small, portable tape recorder, and practiced alone for hours at a time over a period of many weeks. Soon he lost his stutter and became more fluent and forceful. After a while he became even more dynamic in his speaking. His name is Msgr. John O'Sullivan.

A few years later this clergyman was assigned to teach at a leading Catholic university. He was so good in classroom instruction that students soon signed up for his classes three years ahead. The last time I saw him teach he came into the classroom with a stack of about 15 books and pamphlets to quote from. His content, organization, logic, quips, and stories were as powerful an attraction as his delivery.

Never forget that content and delivery are siamese twins. You need as much preparation and practice on the content as on the delivery to be successful. Famous lecturer and former radio news commentator, Lowell Thomas, suggests that speakers use a short formula: "The shortcut to effective speaking is enlarged conversation." By "enlarged conversation" he does not mean that you should sound as though you were on a soapbox, or scold, preach, or talk down to people, but rather that you should converse with your listeners in an audible yet personal, conversational style.

Another good point to remember is that it's never too late for you to start to improve and become a fine speaker. The world-famous actor, John Barrymore, did not take acting seriously until he was 36 years old. He wanted to be an artist. At that time he had a heavy Brooklyn accent, but he studied voice and diction and practiced studiously. You know the rest of the story. He became one of the greatest actors of all time.

Again, age is not a drawback; in fact, it should be an asset. Older people have more experiences to draw from and presumably more knowledge. As Henry Ford once remarked, "The secret of success is getting started." And he wasn't referring to starting cars. He meant getting into action yourself. After all, you can start practicing today. So let's list some ideal ways to learn or improve your speech. Use whatever types of rehearsing appeal to you.

TWELVE SECRETS FOR PRACTICING YOUR SPEECH

Not all of the methods I will discuss are secrets to everybody. Speakers, teachers, and actors use these techniques regularly. Perhaps this is the key to becoming more professional or polished: regular practice and constant evaluation of yourself by anyone you can get to listen to you—your spouse or children, colleagues or neighbors, or any audience at a club, meeting, or organization who will listen to you. Always get them to give you oral and written critiques, since it's easier to improve when you know exactly which things you need to work on the most.

Let's review some of the ways I've already mentioned for practicing. A tape recorder is easy to use and is an excellent method. You can read something from a book or a magazine into the tape recorder and work on improving your vocal variety and speaking style. Be your own judge as to how you can improve by trying different techniques: be more enthusiastic, speak faster, speak slower, speak up more, or speak more quietly. Again, get someone to critique the recording. You could put the tape recorder in the back of a room or at a distance from you if you are practicing outdoors. Set the volume up a bit and fire away. This exercise should also force you to speak up and project your voice.

It takes energy and force to talk to larger groups, even with a microphone. A microphone can't give you vitality, force, or vocal variety; the speaker still has to do the work. The microphone only amplifies. Don't be too soft or too casual. Speak up and speak out. Use gestures, for they will add color to your speaking. After all, you want to emphasize the positive and acquire good speaking habits. You don't want to continue using negative habits. Getting enthusiastic about your subject and your speaking is essential even for practicing. Later, also get excited about your audience. Use full gestures and vital ones.

Another excellent device to help you practice is the videotape recorder. If you can't rent a unit take a course where you can see and hear yourself and be your own best critic. You may not believe or act upon the advice of others, but when you see and hear yourself giving speeches a few times you'll know what to do to improve. The instructor and fellow classmembers will also suggest improvements you can make.

The easiest way to get before a camera is to take a college course, an adult education course, or a course at the American Management Association in cities across the country. But make sure the speech course uses videotape. You will learn and improve faster if you see yourself in action a few times. You may look 10 pounds heavier on camera and you will not like your voice, but these two quirks are true of everyone, even the professionals. The idea is to get busy and change things for the better.

Besides those two modern, electronic means of practicing, audio and videotaping, you can do any of the following for practice and development. Speak to yourself in front of a mirror. This works well for many people. I've never liked this technique as well as the others, because there is no audience. An audience of just one is at least a live audience, so talk to just one individual seated in front of you and pretend you're talking to many. Of course, if you gather the family together, you'll have a larger group to challenge you. Try your speech or just a few stories or jokes on anyone who'll listen to you. And always ask for an evaluation —good points as well as suggestions for improvement.

You can do as many speakers do and practice in an empty auditorium. A microphone isn't necessary, but use one if it's available. It's best to work at projecting your voice naturally. Speak out to the rear wall in the room or go outdoors and talk to the birds and the trees.

The late Charles Laughton, a brilliant actor and a dynamic speaker, practiced speaking by reading out loud to himself, his family, or anyone visiting. He said the family did this regularly with each member taking a turn at reading stories and even interpreting them dramatically. Mr. Laughton eventually wound up doing these readings to packed auditoriums at universities and conventions. I've found it to be a great way to make use of your reading time. You will be making double use of your time: you will learn by hearing as well as by seeing. If you read from newspapers or magazines it's a good way to practice and catch up on the day's news at the same time.

Don't overlook becoming a lector in your church or volunteering to become an officer in the PTA, church, synagogue, or service organizations such as the Elks, Moose, Knights of Columbus, Shriners, Junior Chamber of Commerce, and Chamber of Commerce to name a few. Become a spokesperson, chairperson, moderator, or officer and get loads of practice. Many professional speakers got started by getting the practice and the confidence necessary from just such an organization.

Force yourself to speak up on issues large or small in meetings and discussions you are already attending at your job or in the community. In this way you will get regular practice without having to join any new clubs or societies. This is also how many speakers moved into the limelight of politics, officerships, professional speaking, preaching, acting, or entertaining. Comedian actor Jackie Mason first studied to be a rabbi. The training for teaching and preaching developed his ability to speak and relate to people.

Another method I prefer is to try a speech out on a smaller audience before I go before the actual audience to talk. I've spoken for clubs and organizations of all kinds free to get experience and also to try out, preview, and get feedback on a speech I plan to give to a huge audience later. I have a friend who conducts a sales school in the evenings 1 mile from my home. I volunteered to speak to a group of 50 of his salespeople free. I needed one hour. I was literally practicing, polishing, perfecting my speech for an audience of 2000 salespeople the following week.

Now you have eleven methods for practicing and one to go. They are:

1. Use audio cassettes.
2. Use videotape recorders.
3. Take a college or adult education course.
4. Practice your speech while you are looking into a mirror.
5. Find an audience of one or two family members, neighbors, or colleagues to listen to your speech.
6. Read out loud to yourself or to others.
7. Speak in an empty auditorium.
8. Go outdoors, away from people, and talk to the trees or the birds.
9. Become a lector in a church or an officer, chairperson, or moderator in a community, educational, business or church group.
10. Speak up on issues in meetings, clubs, groups, discussions, and conferences that you attend.
11. Preview your speeches before a smaller group somewhere.

I've saved the twelfth until last. It is an ideal way to develop your speaking, thinking, listening, and leadership ability. I suggest you look into Toastmasters International for men and women which has branches all over the world. You'll find clubs where you work and where you live, and even in smaller towns and communities. Many companies and organizations have toastmaster clubs for their own people right on their premises.

Toastmasters International was started in California in the mid-1920s for people to learn to speak effectively. It is a nonprofit organization dedicated to helping people through regular meetings, either weekly or biweekly, to become better speakers, thinkers, and listeners. There are approximately 70,000 members in the world. Some clubs meet at lunchtime or after work. Others meet over dinner or in the early evening after dinner. Some even have early-morning breakfast meetings. You'll find a club to suit you nearby. I've been a member of the organization since 1949 and have belonged to clubs in Wisconsin, Minnesota, and New York.

You will learn by participation at each meeting in a number of ways. Each week someone is asked to prepare to be the Toastmaster or Toastmistress and runs the speaking and evaluation portion of the session. There are usually four speakers each week who give talks that last from five to seven minutes. Just about every member is called upon to comment on an assigned topic in an impromptu talk each week. In some meetings you'll serve either as a general evaluator of the entire meeting or as an evaluator of one of the speakers. Also, every time you give a speech you are evaluated orally and in writing. Each week there is a different assignment.

Once you become a member of Toastmasters International you will receive a manual, which is a basic book on communication and leadership outlining different types of talks you should work on during the first year. Then you can proceed to an advanced speaker level and give other types of talks over the next year.

The costs of belonging to the organization are nominal. The dues are usually about $30 a year, but they may vary with each club according to its charter. The cost of meals depends on what you order if the meeting is held during a mealtime. If the training you receive from the course is related to your job, the training cost would be deductible.

Once you become a member, you are eligible to enter the International Serious Speech Contest in your club, and if you win in the area, division, district, and zone competitions, you could eventually speak in the International finals at the annual convention. The annual Humorous Speech Contest terminates at the district level but still allows you the possibility of winning four contests to become a district champ.

To find out about the organization and clubs that meet in your area, simply drop a card or note to Toastmasters International, Santa Ana, California, 92711. Ask for information and details of clubs that meet in the area where you work and also where you live, if they are two different places. Attend a meeting or two and visit a couple of nearby clubs. It costs you nothing to look and little to belong. The time, effort, and expense will be worthwhile just for the fellowship and ideas gained from others who are there to improve themselves.

The Toastmasters' motto is "The future belongs to the people who prepare." You'll learn by doing and you'll have a lot of fun. As for age, there are no requirements.

HOW TO REMEMBER WITHOUT MEMORIZING

The best way to recall the main points of a speech is to form a mental picture of each of the key ideas in your speech. I've used this method for many years. Although I recommend that you prepare an outline for effective, confident, and organized speaking, it's best to be able to get along without any notes so the alternative is to use mental pictures or symbols.

For example, in a speech I used to give on human relations, my opening was a quotation by John D. Rockefeller, Sr.: "The ability to deal with people is as purchasable as sugar and coffee, and I'll pay more for that ability than any other quality on earth." To recall that quotation, I would form a mental picture of money, sugar or coffee, or even Rockefeller giving money away. What could be easier? Once I had formed that mental picture a question would come to mind. "Does it really pay big dividends to practice good human relations?" The proof that this method works well is that I haven't given that talk for 10 years but it all comes back to me because of that mental picture.

Continuing now with my human relations speech, I now use a mental picture of *Reader's Digest* and the figure 70 percent. This then reminds me of a survey the magazine took of major corporations, in which they asked, "Of the last 25 people fired from your company, what were the reasons?" In 70 percent of the cases the reason was this one: "their inability to get along with their fellow employees." So now I add to my speech, "We can see that human relations pays big dividends. Our jobs, friendships, and income depend on this ability." Then I say, "Now I propose a four-point program to improve our human relations ability." All I've needed so far to tell them spontaneously everything up to this point were mental pictures of: money or coffee, a question, *Reader's Digest*, and 70 percent (or *Reader's Digest* opened to page 70 showing people in a welfare line, out of work; or Rockefeller giving out money, which reminds me of the quotation and the question that follows).

The heart of the talk is the easiest part of all to recall if you outline it mentally and perhaps develop one or more themes for it. In this particular example (human relations) my first theme is made up of four points as listed above, each with supporting stories, quotes and incidents. My second theme is money so my four points spell out "cash," but I will keep this until last to hold the audience's interest and to provide suspense. In fact, when I get through, you'll see that you can recall my entire speech by thinking of the word "cash" or of a picture of a dollar sign as the "s" in "cash" and a question mark following. For added assurance you could have it appear on page 70 of *Reader's Digest* (70 percent fired for poor human relations).

The four points in this talk were the following.

1. Don't criticize, condemn, or complain—three "c's" but easy to recall with one "c." For supporting data I would use a story about Abe

Lincoln. The word "cash" recalls Lincoln because he returned a couple of pennies to a store, but he also talked about curbing criticism, so that word, which is a key point, reminds me of his famous saying, "with malice toward none, with charity towards all."

2. Give honest, sincere appreciation. "Appreciation" is the key word, so that's the "a" in "cash." I would add a Mark Twain quotation here. "I can live for two months on a good compliment," so "appreciation" reminds me of his saying. Other supporting data can be tied in just as easily. I can give this complete speech in approximately two minutes as I've outlined it for you or by adding more stories, anecdotes, and quotes, I can talk easily for an hour on the four points. But most of our talks will be five to ten minutes.

3. Become sincerely interested in other people. I use "s" for "sincerely interested" because it's so essential that the friendship be genuine and sincere. It's easy now to recall the great statesman Bernard Baruch's observation, "You can win more friends in two months by showing sincere interest in others, than you can in two years by trying to interest others in you."

4. Have a hearty enthusiasm. I feel that ordinary energy and enthusiasm aren't enough, so I use the "h" to represent "hearty." There are endless quotations on enthusiasm and I would use a few of these. One is Longfellow's three words, "Enthusiasm begets enthusiasm." Another is a quote by Frank Bettcher, former major league baseball player and top insurance salesperson for years, "Act enthusiastic and you'll be enthusiastic."

Until this moment my audience would not know that I have spelled "cash" with these four points. I would ask them at the end of each point to picture a huge neon sign flashing on and off: one of a giant "c" after the first point; one of a giant "ca" after the second point; and a third of a giant "cas" after the third point. When I finish my fourth point, probably they would be wondering what "case" means, because automatically they would have added the "e" from "enthusiasm." But I would then say "hearty" is a key word so let's use the "h" to represent "hearty enthusiasm." And now I would ask, "What does that spell?" The audience would shout back "cash." Then I would say, "So you see, it really does pay to practice good human relations."

Now, "cash" also reminds me of my closing. I have people set to help me. I say, "Now to remind you to use these four points to keep your job and income, to win more friends, and to have more fun, I'm having a brand new copper plaque of Abraham Lincoln presented to each one of you. It's a brand new penny. It will serve to remind you of the "cash" principles." I've already quoted Lincoln and told about Rockefeller giving out new dimes, so for a laugh I say, "I can't afford to give out new dimes, so you'll have to settle for the Lincoln penny." That brings a laugh and I'm through.

If I gave that human relations talk as I just outlined it for you in mental pictures, it would take just two or three minutes. It's easy to tell stories or incidents to tie in with your key points as supporting evidence. I used only quotations in my example, however, I often use stories as well.

In summary, never memorize a speech word for word. It's a sure way to dullness or failure, or both. But always know your opening and closing by heart. In this way you won't forget these two vital areas, and you can concentrate on being friendly, confident, and positive and on looking at your audience.

Most professional speakers use a memory system. I'm suggesting this simplest and easiest one of forming mental pictures to use as a beginning. I sometimes use notes, but more often I prefer this way. A great speaker, Bishop Sheen, once remarked: "You or I have no right to take up an audience's time if we can't speak for at least one-half hour without using notes."

THE ART OF USING NOTES EFFECTIVELY

To again quote Bishop Sheen, "I first write out my speech. Then I tear it up. Then I write it out again and once more I tear it up. Now I write an outline and give the final speech from that outline." I've long advocated the same technique used by Bishop Sheen. I suggest working from a simple outline when you speak. I suggest using 8 × 10 cards or a simple file-folder cut in two. Don't use paper, because it's difficult to handle and too flimsy. It also rattles when the speaker moves and sounds like a forest fire through the microphone.

I print in skeleton outline the essential key words or phrases in big, clear, block letters, including subheadings for supporting data, on four or five cards (rather than crowding everything on one or two cards). For shorter speeches under 15 minutes I use no more than two large cards.

Besides not rattling into a sensitive microphone, cards are easy to handle and easy to see and read from, especially if large printing has been used. Notes should not be seen and should be put on the lectern out of sight. Any aid should be hidden until it is used. Also, nothing should be in the speaker's hands at all unless a visual aid or a pointer is being used. The only reason a speaker would pick up a card would be to quote someone, to read statistics correctly, or perhaps to read a short poem. However, it's best to memorize poems and quotations. Reading notes can block direct communication and can curb spontaneity.

For effective speech communication notes that are properly

prepared and handled are a definite asset. They will help you to speak only on your prepared material and will help you to avoid rambling. Also, notes will help you not to "go blank" as every speaker does occasionally, because you can simply glance at your outline and continue unflustered.

To show you how this technique works in detail let's refer back to the human relations speech I outlined earlier. Here's how we would develop a written outline for the same speech. The outline would use key words, symbols, or pictures in the form of drawings, or the first words of key phrases. Using a large 8 × 10 card you would list the key words in this order: "Rockefeller quote" or "the ability to deal. . . ." Then below this on two successive lines you would write "Question: Does it really pay . . . , etc.?" and "*Reader's Digest*, page 70." On the next line you would write the first point, "Don't criticize." Underneath that and indented you would write, "Abe Lincoln Story." Any other supporting data would be placed directly under that.

Then you would print point number two, "Give appreciation." Indented under that you would write the first point, "Mark Twain quote" or the first words of the quotation "I can live for. . . ." You would write the third point next as "Become sincerely interested" and indented under that the words, "Bernard Baruch," or the first words of his observation, "You can win. . . ."

Finally, you would write point number four, "Have a hearty enthusiasm," and indented underneath the supporting data, "Longfellow; Frank Bettcher." Then you would have the summary "CASH" and the closing "new pennies distributed." You would fill in the rest of the talk spontaneously as you go. It's not memorized, it's organized, and it's concise. Again, I've kept this example brief and simple to illustrate the form of the outline.

TECHNIQUES FOR TIMING

Here is one more recommendation about writing the outline. Leave space on one side of the outline for you to write in how long you should have talked at certain points. This would only apply to speeches longer than five minutes, but it can be done for shorter speeches. When you practice and rehearse the speech, note how long you've spoken at key points. Then write those figures in the appropriate spaces next to the outline so you can see whether you are running long or on time. There's nothing wrong with finishing ahead of time, but most speakers don't. Therefore, the time periods written on the outline will help you avoid speaking for too long a time. This technique is excellent if you are writing an outline, but if you are using a mental outline for your speech instead, you need another method. One of these is used by Lavain G. Bue, an outstanding speaker and speech teacher in San Mateo, California. He has a large special wristwatch with an alarm. He sets the alarm to go off at two or three minutes before the end of the time he's been allowed. When the alarm goes off into the microphone it startles the audience and he says, "Whoops! My time is almost up so I'll close. He then goes into his closing and the audience loves it.

Another technique for finishing a speech on time or ahead of time is suggested by Bud Hogberg, a speaker and businessman from Newport Beach, California. Bud says, "Have a droppable unit, a droppable module that won't ruin your talk or won't be missed if it's left out." Of course you would never omit or rush the closing of a speech, so every wise speaker should know the opening and closing by heart and also know how long the closing takes. If the speech is running long, Hogberg drops a unit or module of data and goes into the closing. He always knows before he begins what can be left out of his speech without hurting it so that he can leave it out if he's running long. Most speakers plan a short speech but run long. You'll find that the longer you're in the speaking business, the harder it is to stop speaking, but time is of the essence so remember to always be as brief as possible. If there's a question and answer period following the speech, you can work in the points you've left out earlier.

I've often used Hogberg's technique successfully, but I add one feature. I always ask the chairperson or director of the event to give me a signal three minutes, before the end of my speech. I tell her or him to make sure I see the signal. It works for me. There's nothing more professional than timing so do what works best for you to keep on time or even finish ahead of time.

HOW THE PROFESSIONALS INVOLVE THE AUDIENCE

Repeating an earlier quotation, "People don't care unless they share." So get your audience involved; let them participate. Asking for a show of hands in answer to questions you ask the audience is more interesting than asking rhetorical questions. Using visuals involves the audience. Question and answer sessions also are excellent participation opportunities. Also look for other ways to give the audience a chance to participate, to be involved, to give their own ideas, or to have more fun.

Sales trainers look for ways to get their salespeople motivated through involvement. I'm sure you've heard of the manager who puts a few $5 bills under some chairs and tells the sales people to pick up their chairs and see who are the lucky ones. The punch line is, "You've got to get off your seats to make money!" It serves as a good warmup and a motivator and it points up a key lesson for salespeople: Don't sit around—it takes more calls to make more sales.

A few weeks ago just before I was to give an hour address to a sales congress in Toronto, Canada, I was given a good idea by a colleague of mine, Bob Sullivan, a sales and public relations consultant in New York City. He reminded me of the old warmup for radio and TV audiences, which I then used. I thanked the chairperson and said, "Good afternoon!" Then I said,"I'm sure you are all acquainted with the people sitting next to you but how about getting acquainted briefly with some others. As soon as I say 'Go,' I want each of you to turn around and shake hands with the person directly behind you. 'Go!' "

The 2000 people all turned around to shake hands with the person right behind them, but there was no one facing them since everyone had turned to the back. People in the last row were actually looking at the back wall. Everyone laughed and a few groaned a little, but the exercise worked as a warmup and was a fun opener.

I continued to involve them by immediately asking the question, "How do you feel?" They shouted back, "Great!" Then I asked another question: "What do you do when you're out selling and you don't feel so great? Or when you feel tired, lazy, bored, even depressed, what do you do to become stimulated, motivated, and excited again?" Usually someone then says, "I give myself a pep talk!" and I respond, "Right! That's the best way! It's also the cheapest, easiest, and quickest way to get instant motivation."

I then ask the audience another question: "When is the best time to give yourself a pep talk?" Now the answers come fast. They cry out, "When you get up!" I say, "When's another time?" And the answers come from salespeople with years of experience, hardship, and success: "when you lose a sale"; "when you make a sale"; "before a call"; "after a call"; "when you go to bed at the end of the day." They are all 100 percent correct and I tell them so.

I don't lecture to them or preach. I use the question and answer method for participation. In this way we all learn together, and we all have fun learning. They often say things that are new and different and that I haven't even thought of.

Four or five short participation opportunities in an hour would be enough (this means one every 10 minutes or so). Stunts or games are excellent to use in the opening and closing and also as devices to wake up the audience in the middle of the speech. Fifteen minutes into my Toronto speech I had an audience member act out a sales role playing situation with me, and half-way through the speech I asked questions of individuals in the audience. In the closing I got them all on their feet and had them exchange a pep talk with one other person. Then I taught them three short pep talks and ended by having them all say together, "Act enthusiastic and you'll be enthusiastic."

When I teach executives I get them involved in exercises to practice better listening techniques, communication games, problem solving partnerships, and small group discussions. I use most of these techniques with any size audience in my speeches as well.

Some famous communication games or exercises include asking someone to turn their back to you and tell you how to put on the suit-jacket you just took off and have in your hands. Of the 100 times I've used this exercise in the last 20 years only about two people have ever been able to do it. Invariably, the volunteer gives technical, complex, and confusing instructions. One fellow said, "Lay your jacket down on the floor opened up with the inside face up. Sit down at a 45-degree angle to it. Now put it on." The listener, following the instructions, had it on upside down and inside out. Keep it simple. Just say, "Put it on the way you always do."

Another participation technique is *brainstorming*. This involves your asking the audience to offer possible solutions, suggestions, or ideas for any problem or question. Often this approach will enrich the experience of everyone. Other methods include using subgroups or teams of two to six people to discuss ideas, written exercises, and role playing.

One speaker years ago asked his audience to stand up at the end of his talk. For his closing he said, "I know you're all stiff from sitting so long and tired and warm, so please stand up. Everyone please raise both arms high above your head and wiggle all your fingers energetically for 15 seconds." When they sat down they were stimulated, more energetic, and smiling. They loved getting into action. An audience will do just about anything you ask within reason, and they'll appreciate you much more for getting them involved. Remember, I'm suggesting using just a few participation possibilities in a speech of one-half an hour to an hour. There should be less participation activity in a shorter talk and more in a longer talk.

CHAPTER 6

Secrets for Successful Impromptu Speaking

KEY STEPS TO ASSURE CONFIDENCE FOR IMPROMPTU SPEAKING

Impromptu speaking, saying something specific and constructive on the spur of the moment, is truly an art. But just like the art of prepared speaking, instant or impromptu eloquence is also an acquirement, not a gift.

People who speak even occasionally know the value of the Boy Scouts' motto: "Be prepared!" Every good speaker should always be ready on sudden notice with a "hip pocket talk" or an inspiring invocation. I include invocation because guest speakers are often called upon without warning to "Please give our invocation." Having one memorized could save you from terrible embarrassment. If you do a poor job giving an invocation, you've lost your audience before you even start your prepared speech.

Here's one sample of a standard invocation (but one in your own words would be even better). Keep this one for emergencies: "Lord, we ask you for your blessing on this gathering and this meal. Let the work of this meeting and the fellowship it brings enable each of us to live better, serve better, and follow Thee more faithfully, Amen."

Concerning the "hip pocket talk," always have an outline handy in a pocket notebook or a billfold. It may not fit every occasion unless you have one that will appeal to everyone. Some themes that suit all ages include how to save money; how to live better and longer; and getting along with others.

When you are called upon to "say a few words," you are never just saying a few words but are revealing a human personality. The best subject matter for talking impromptu is to speak from your own experience. The *core* of your speaking should revolve around what you've learned through conversation, observation, reading, and experience. The best of these is experience; nothing quite compares with an incident that actually occurred—an experience or incident out of your life that is appropriate to the audience and the occasion. Everybody loves nostalgia, so reminisce a little. Don't make anything up. Stick to the truth and always be as accurate as possible.

At a banquet for salespeople I was called upon by surprise to give a little speech. I stood up, greeted the group, and said, "I'll never forget the first real job I had when I was 11 years old. Real sales expertise was involved in it too. A new newspaper had just started publication in my hometown. It was the third paper, an evening paper. I had a grand total of 39 customers on 39 blocks. It was tough getting people to buy the paper, *The Minneapolis Star*, in 1939. It was a breeze on a bicycle in the summertime, but during the cold, snowy winters in Minnesota, the trudging by foot through heavy drifts of snow for nearly 4 miles of delivering and selling took real stamina. I've been forever grateful that I persisted and kept that route. It taught me a lesseon for life that has paid off many times since. The lesson is this: be persistent; never give up; persist until you succeed. This applies to every kind of work but especially to selling, where rejection is a daily occurrence. Let's all work harder to do better in the year ahead. Even if there isn't an award for you for superior work at this event next year, you'll be able to take pride in the fact that you did your best.

"Remember the stirring words of Winston Churchill spoken to the youngsters at the Harrow School in England. Churchill was revisiting the site of his early education. He looked out at the faces of the students and said nine words: 'Never give up! Never, never, never, never, never, never!' "

My few words took just one and one-half minutes and I was given an ovation. The fact is I had never given the talk before. I had used the Churchill quote before, but the rest was spontaneous. It also was appropriate to the occasion and to the audience, people who must persist everyday to succeed in selling on commission only. It met the criteria for impromptu talks: short, specific, spirited. I was able to do well because I followed the *"core"* idea mentioned earlier in this chapter. I had read and previously used the quotation. I remembered the experience when I thought of selling and hard work. Fortunately the paper route incident popped into my mind.

You'll always do well if you remember one incident. One example or one experience is all you need to do well. Your experiences could include work, family, school, hobbies, interests, sports, religion, accidents, awards, success, and failures. You have also your likes and dislikes, peeves and pet peeves, pets, clothing, jewelry, mottos, favorite songs, food, drinks, political convictions, travels, and perhaps even secret ambitions. The scope is wide; the list is practically endless. Your only chore is to pick an idea, incident, or subject quickly and speak on it. Make your point and back it up with some examples. Limit your topic. This is especially important when you're called upon to say "just a few words."

FOUR METHODS FOR ORGANIZING INSTANTLY ON ANY TOPIC

Rudyard Kipling, the great author of many classic stories such as *Kim* and *The Man Who Would Be King*, provides our first technique for organized impromptu speaking. Kipling revealed the method in answer to the question, "How are you able to be so prolific as a writer?" Kipling's answer was, "I have six honest servants. They've taught me all I know. Their names are who, what, when, where, why, and how." So in six words you have the rudiments of all good speaking, writing, and reporting. You will always be successful—specific, organized, and concise—using this formula. You will also be more interesting.

Here's how it should work. Pick any incident out of your life and apply the "six honest servants." As an example, suppose you have a scar on your hand. You would answer the questions, "What happened," "When, where, who was involved," "How did it happen," "Why did it happen?" And there must be a moral to the story. The answers would be as follows. "When I was about eight years old the family went on a picnic to the local zoo." In this first sentence you've already answered "who, what, when, and where."

Next you would say, "We were looking into the monkey cage at some cute little monkeys. One sign read Don't climb over the fence! But I did climb over it. Another sign warned, Don't feed the monkeys! But I wanted to touch the monkeys, so I reached my hand into the cage and tried to pet one of them. The monkey bit my little finger between his teeth and I screamed, Help! People reached through the fence and pulled me back but they almost ripped my little finger off in getting me free of the monkey. "This answers "how" and "why."

To end you might say, "I still have the scar to remind me to always obey signs." You've now provided a moral to the story, which also is a natural ending. Using Kipling's method will assure clarity, conciseness, specificity, and organization. It is absolutely the best formula for speaking and writing that I've ever found.

The second best method I've found for effective impromptu speaking is an excellent formula for prepared speaking as well. I believe credit for originating the method should go to June Guncheon Vajda, a highly successful speech teacher. It's called the "PREP" formula. Of course PREP serves as an abbreviation for "prepared" or "preparation." I've used this method for years, and I've taught it to thousands of people in speech courses. It has saved me many times in surprise impromptu situations. I've even won speech contests using the formula.

The first "P" is for "point": State your point. The "R" is for "reason": Have a reason for your point. The "E" is for "example": Give just one example. An example can be in the form of a statistic, comparison, incident or experience, illustration, or exhibit or demonstration. Any talk without a concrete example is weak. The final "P" is for "point": Restate or paraphrase your point or position. What could be easier to remember: "point," "reason," "example," "point"?

Let's apply the PREP formula to the same human relations speech that I used as an example in the previous chapter. Here's how it would come out.

My point is: "Develop your ability to deal with people to be successful as a manager."

My reason is: "A manager's job is to get things done through people. Managers succeed only if their subordinates succeed. Human relations ability is essential to direct and to motivate others."

My example is: "According to a *Reader's Digest* survey of top corporations, 70 percent of people fired from their jobs are fired because of their inability to get along with their peers. However, the ability to deal with people can be developed."

"Benjamin Franklin was tactless in his youth but worked on his human relations' faults and weaknesses one at a time throughout the year. He listed 13 faults at the start of the year and worked on each one for four weeks straight. He became an expert in handling people. He even served as an ambassador to France for nine years when he was in his seventies."

My final point is: "You'll be a more successful manager by sharpening your human relations ability through study and practice just as Ben Franklin did."

It takes only one minute or less to give this complete talk based on the PREP formula. Test yourself right now. Take any controversial subject on crime, welfare, communism, unemployment, or abortion, for example, and apply the PREP formula to develop a short talk instantly on that subject. You'll do remarkably better if you follow the formula than if you do not.

Although I have suggested using the PREP formula in this chapter as an excellent method for impromptu speaking, note that I used an illustration from a prepared speech on human relations and adapted it slightly. The point is this: the formula works well for any talk, but it is a magic formula for the time you are challenged to be instantly eloquent.

Another formula for impromptu excellence is the "Past, Present, Future" method. It applies to every animate or inanimate person or thing you could mention. Again, the rules of impromptu speaking apply; be specific, brief, and organized and have a topic appropriate to the audience and the occasion.

Let's suppose you are called upon to speak suddenly at a gathering of airline pilots or flight attendants, cab drivers, or railroad engineers and conductors. The subject of prominence is transportation. If you quickly apply the "past, present, future" formula to transportation, the words will come out almost automatically.

> "Ages ago in the distant *past* people had to walk everywhere they went. Consequently, they didn't go far away from their place of birth.
>
> "Our *present* transportation, in contrast, particularly jets, can whiz us across the ocean to another continent in less than four hours.
>
> "What does the *future* hold? Already in the news are the U.S. space-shuttle experiments, which will allow us in the near future to spend a vacation or even go to work on another planet. Are you ready to sign up? Or will you settle for the predicted fast travel just a little off the ground that may come sooner? I'm talking about monorails for mass transportation, which will move safely at high speeds. We'll soon have our pick."

See how easy it is?

Here is another method for successful impromptu challenges. In brief, it is called "Use an object or a visual aid"—the show-and-tell idea. For example, a scar on your hand provides an exhibit, a visual aid. If you are pressed to "say a few words," you might have an item, article, poem, quotation, gadget or motto on your person, in your wallet, or in a briefcase that you have with you. Don't overlook a chance to use something visual and don't miss the opportunity to pull something out of your pocket or purse and talk about it. You'll find it helps in getting out of a pressured situation.

Sometimes I have in my pocket a marble that has a gold band around that says, "Do unto others as you would have them do unto you." I've used it several times to introduce a short talk when I am called upon unexpectedly. Also, I have my briefcase with me always. In it I have brochures, pens, pencils, cards, medicines, a pointer (the collapsible kind), a checkbook, a Henny Youngman pocket jester in the form of a tape measure with 45 one-liners printed on it, plus a round tuit, which is a round piece of plastic about the size of a quarter. It reminds me to *"get around to it"* instead of procrastinating. All of these things are visual and all are good potential subjects for developing a short talk. I've been an instant comedy hit with the pocket jester.

Further, my billfold in my jacket pocket contains eight credit cards, four or five association cards, club cards, a list of short pep talks, some money, business cards of recent days, snapshots, and even a couple of fortune cookie quotations that I've saved. I also found a quotation by Thoreau that came out of a Cracker Jack box awhile back: "Men were born to succeed, not fail." Every one of these items can be the substance and the exhibit for a talk.

I have devised an adaptation of the "Use an object or a visual aid" method. It's the acronym "SPEECH." "S" stands for "Subject"; "P" is for "Point"; "E" is for "Enthusiasm"; "E" is for "Exhibit"; "C" is for "Concise" (or "Clarity"); and "H" is for "Humor." All you really need is an object for the exhibit and the rest will come easily. You make a point about it concisely, clearly, and enthusiastically. It's clearer of course because you have a visual aid, something to show as you talk about it. And you try to work humor into talk. If you pick a funny item, such as the round tuit I have, the humor automatically will be the object.

Now you have four formulas that will help make your speaking, especially the impromptu kind, more successful. One of the four should fit any situation you find yourself challenged by.

PITFALLS TO AVOID

The first pitfall to avoid in speaking is: Never apologize. The only exception would be if you were late for an engagement. Then you would apologize, profusely. Audiences don't want to hear you tell them you aren't prepared, you aren't qualified, or you aren't feeling well. They'll find out these things soon enough. An apology is dull and boring and, in addition, it detracts from you as a speaker and as a person.

Another pitfall to avoid is: Don't be too general in your speaking.

Audiences are interested in stories, experiences, and details, not assumptions, guesses, prologues, presumptions, or generalities. Generalities are the refuge of a weak mind. Be specific.

Here is an example of a speech that is packed with trite, dull, worn clichés. It says nothing because it doesn't contain an example and is not specific. Yet, many speakers, even prepared ones, speak in such boring general terms as these. Remember, this is an example of how *not* to speak.

> "My friends, as we travel the long road ahead down to the grass roots of our city, there are these extremists whose voices cry out in the night, We must not forsake, but rather, with wisdom recall that there are those who say tomorrow may be too late. Make no mistake—in our overall approach no one will dispute this fact—and it is a sobering thought.
>
> "It is more perhaps than coincidence and honesty demands, whether we desire it or not, that we face up to the issue. This observation has led me to one conclusion.
>
> "Where then, shall we turn? In my judgment I do not wish to confuse the issue. My primary aim has always been to understand the problem better. I do not pretend to know the answers. There are unmistakable signs, I submit to you. And in such a view we are perhaps more to be applauded than condemned, as the world may one day see.
>
> "It has been a distinct honor and privilege. And in conclusion let me reiterate once again what words cannot express. On that note, may I leave you with this parting thought, which I know will be taken in the spirit in which it is offered, for the die is cast. Thank you!"

There are so many clichés in one short talk. It's a talk that may please everyone but says nothing. In the end it probably will please no one. Being specific avoids many pitfalls, including an aimless, nervous "Thank you."

You've guessed the next pitfall, I'm sure: Don't ever close a talk with a plain, meaningless "Thank you." Unless you tell the audience why you are thanking them, you risk sounding insincere. If you have informed, inspired, or entertained the audience, when you conclude *they'll thank you* with applause. Why are you thanking the audience? If you know why, tell them specifically. Don't expect them to guess. And don't ruin the most important part of the talk, the closing, with a dull "Thank you."

On the other hand, you can thank people profusely when you are introduced or you can thank them specifically for their time or response or for listening before you close your talk. But always use your well-prepared closing to end the talk.

Also, a simple "Thank you" after you've received a gift or an award is fine, since it's obvious what you are saying "Thank you" for.

Perhaps the worst pitfall of all in either prepared or impromptu speaking is to talk too long, to run overtime, and to get carried away. By keeping your talks short, you can save time for your listeners and for yourself. And brevity is the soul of clarity. Samuel Johnson advised, "A person who uses a great many words to express the meaning of something is like a bad marksman who, instead of aiming a single stone at an object, takes up a handful and throws it in hopes of hitting it."

The story is told of the man who wrote a long letter to his nephew. At the end he added this postscript: "Pardon me for writing such a long letter. I didn't have time to write a short one."

If you talk too long, someone might get up and recite this poem: "Now I sit me down to sleep, the speaker is dull, the subject is deep; if he should stop before I wake, give me a poke for goodness sake."

Another pitfall of the impromptu speaker is to be too lackluster, which often is a direct result of not being totally prepared, speaking too softly or too slowly. A weak voice is a sign of fear. So get excited, speak up, and speak out. Use gestures and make the words live. By the way, speaking too slowly or too softly is often a common problem of prepared speakers as well as unprepared speakers. Speakers must speak faster and louder than people do in ordinary conversation. People listen four to eight times as fast as the average person speaks, so don't bore them. Keep it lively.

You'll have more spirit in your voice if you use some gestures for emphasis and description. I've noticed that many impromptu speakers lack animation. They are concentrating so hard on thinking of their message that they forget to get excited and therefore have few gestures. Gestures help to put the speaker at ease as well as to keep the audience's interest. Make only meaningful gestures, however. Don't overdo it, but keep from being a statue. Action cures fears.

I'm frequently asked, "What about walking during the talk—is it acceptable?" The answer is, "Yes, but don't walk aimlessly. Walk only with purpose, like a lawyer in court who appeals to the jury, then walks toward the defendant, then towards the judge. Always move with a purpose."

Movement could be effective for changing the pace or for getting closer to the audience (or one segment of the audience). You could move from one side of the stage to the other but don't look down while you are walking. Keep your eyes on the audience at all times if possible. It will defeat your purpose if you walk aimlessly and are looking at the wall, ceiling, or floor while you are walking. Look into the eyes and faces of the members of the audience. Look directly at one person at a time and dwell on that person's face for a few seconds. Then look at someone else.

Again, walking is distracting unless it is done with purpose. Obviously anything that doesn't add detracts. Speakers who are challenged to speak in an impromptu situation are prone to walk aimlessly and look at the ceiling for inspiration. Neither will help. They will only breed failure, because a speaker who walks a lot, rocks, or weaves back and forth, is thought to be nervous, disinterested, unprepared, or amateurish.

One of the common faults of all speakers, but especially speakers who are called on by surprise or on short notice, is to fail to smile. Impromptu speakers rarely flash even a hint of a smile. Fool them! Let people think you're happy and not struggling to think of something interesting to say. Most speakers are happy but they fail to notify their face.There's nothing that communicates friendliness and confidence as well as a warm, natural smile. And remember, people are judging you from what they see even before they hear a word from you. A smile shows your desire to communicate with them.

Impromptu speakers are most vulnerable to word-whiskers, boring words such as "Ah," "and ah," "you know," and others. They are known as "aspirated pauses" and detract from a talk. Make your pauses silent and distinct. Give people time to assimilate and comprehend your material. Impromptu and prepared speakers also should get rid of other dull clichés, trite, meaningless phrases such as, "so to speak," "in any event," "and so on and so forth," "whatever," "what have you," "viable," "at this point in time," and "fantastic," to name a few. Banish them from your speech. Find fresh, lively, original words and phrases to make your speech picturesque.

Arnold Bennett, the English novelist, declared, "Many frictions and problems of daily life are caused by abrasive sound, speech habits and mannerisms." We've mentioned the abrasive sounds, but now let's look at another pitfall of speakers, especially unprepared speakers—faulty mannerisms.

The definition of mannerism is, "any habitual peculiarity of manner." Some specific examples are: continually pulling at an ear, rubbing or pulling of the nose, putting hands in pockets, playing with a ring, a watch, a pen or a pencil, a paper clip, or fingering any type of article and distracting the audience. These playthings are called "toys" and should be completely eliminated.

As a rule, you should have nothing in your hands, unless you are using a visual aid or a pointer. Get used to keeping your hands by your sides when you are not using them. Don't hide them or clasp them behind you or in front of you. Don't grab onto one wrist and hang on for dear life. This will curb your naturalness and spontaneity and will communicate fear and nervousness to your audience. And don't kill your chances for success by grabbing onto the lectern as though it were going to fly away.

If you tie your hands down in this way, or any other way, you will be unsuccessful in your speech. Hanging onto the lectern gives the impression of an uncertain, lazy, tired, or unprofessional speaker.

It seems as if there are more pitfalls to think about than there are positive things to do. Actually, all the pitfalls mentioned here are just as likely to be the faults of a prepared speaker as well as an impromptu speaker, but an impromptu speaker is more vulnerable to all of them.

So look over the methods once again for successful impromptu speaking and then read the following suggestions for practicing speaking on the spur of the moment. Apply the various formulas mentioned previously.

HOW TO PRACTICE AND SHARPEN YOUR SPEAKING ABILITY

Besides joining Toastmaster International for regular weekly practice before an audience, as I mentioned previously, there are some techniques you can use to practice on your own and with others during otherwise unproductive times on social occasions or when you are driving in a car on a long trip. I've always found practicing on such occasions as profitable diversions and practical as well as fun.

With one of these techniques you can practice anywhere, anytime. I give credit for this simple but excellent technique to Grace Walsh, a college debating coach from Eau Claire, Wisconsin, who in 1976 was voted by the Debate Society of America the foremost debate coach in the last century in American colleges.

Here's the simple technique for practice. When we were at her home for a Sunday dinner, for example, after dinner she would give each of us on the debating team a one-word topic for speaking impromptu for two minutes. It's excellent training. Any topic is fair game: fork, spoon, cake, plate, candle, tie, chair, sugar, coffee, pork chops, ashtray, and so on. Notice that the topics I mentioned are all concrete, tangible items. A more difficult challenge is to speak on abstract topics such as love, faith, hope, or patriotism.

Try it yourself. Pick a topic and start talking about it as interestingly, colorfully, and specifically as possible. It may be hard at first, but with a little practice you'll soon amaze yourself. You'll learn faster if you experiment with all the formulas explained in detail in the beginning of this chapter. Use a tape recorder to pick up what you say and then play your talk back or use a videotape system, if possible. Time them. Evaluate yourself for organization, logic, specificity, examples, voice, pace, and emphasis. You can do this alone anytime, but it's fun if you take turns with others when they are present. Time and evaluate one another.

When you are driving in a car you can take turns with other members of your family or with friends and challenge one another. Again, use one-word topics of objects you see: cow, telephone pole, train, grass, corn, barn, tree. Always try to speak for at least one minute and say something constructive. In time, you'll become so fluent that people will wonder how you did it.

Later on, when you're together with a group, perhaps your family, or friends, have them challenge you to one-sentence topics. And you also challenge those who want to practice speaking impromptu. Use topics such as "how I got into my line of work"; "my hobby and how I became interested in it"; "my hometown and what I like or don't like about it"; "my greatest handicap"; "my secret ambition." Again, limit the length of your talk to one or two minutes.

One other idea for polishing your impromptu talks is to pick up an object and talk about it for a minute or so. Get in the habit of thinking about using visual aids. Your listeners will expect visual aids because of the impact of TV in their lives. Always try to exhibit or demonstrate what you are talking about.

Because attitude is so important for your success in any kind of speaking, but especially unprepared speaking, you should learn this quotation by Oliver Wendell Holmes: "Success is the result of mental attitude, and the right mental attitude will bring success in everything you do."

Finally, keep in mind that there are two kinds of preparation: remote and proximate. Proximate is what you do to immediately get ready to speak or from the time you learn about a talk and the time you give it. This type of preparation is rarely helpful in an impromptu situation. Remote preparation is your biggest help for impromptu speaking and perhaps for prepared speaking as well. Remember the story about the scar on my hand that I wrote about earlier. It happened to me when I was eight years old. That's over 40 years ago, but I recall every detail of the scene. So, I was preparing to give that talk for over 40 years. We all have a treasury of experiences buried in our memories. If you tap these experiences, you'll always be prepared.

A final thought on preparation, the key to self-confidence, enthusiasm, and competence. The words I would like you to remember are those of the great Prime Minister of England, Lloyd George:

> To trust to the inspiration of the moment—that is the fatal phase upon which many promising careers have been wrecked. The surest road to inspiration is preparation. I have seen many men and women of courage and capacity fail for lack of industry. Mastery in speech comes from mastery in one's subject.

His last sentence is an important one. Mastery comes from study and practice or in a word: preparation.

I've written about a lot of pitfalls for speakers and the solutions for eliminating or avoiding them. In all truthfulness, there is just one sure cure for all of the negative speech habits, weaknesses, faults, foibles, and affected mannerisms: *Get truly excited on the right subject and 99 percent of the faults of your speaking will disappear.*

CHAPTER 7

Professional Tips for Answering Questions and Objections

===

TIPS FOR ANSWERING QUESTIONS FROM THE AUDIENCE

If a question and answer period follows a speech, which more and more audiences want today, the speech isn't over until the last question is answered and the speaker sits down. Many speakers do superbly well on their prepared speech and then ruin the occasion by doing a poor job of answering questions. You can avoid doing poorly, however, if you keep the following points in mind.

1. Concentrate on the individual who is asking the question, and look directly at that person. Don't pick up your notes or play with anything. Have nothing in your hands at all. Show complete interest in the person and in the question being asked.

2. Listen for both the content and the intent. Notice the facial expression and body language of the questioner. Listen for the tone of voice, a clue to the person's feelings. In short, listen for what is being asked and interpret what is meant by the question. Listening between the lines sometimes helps understand the intent of the questioner better.

3. Acknowledge the question when the audience is large. Repeat

the question if the questioner cannot be heard by all. Ordinarily you will have a microphone, but the people asking questions will not have one and cannot be heard by everyone, so remember to repeat the question if it's necessary.

4. Ask for clarification of the question if it isn't clear. Perhaps paraphrase the question back to the individual and ask if that is correct.

5. Answer the question clearly, specifically, and briefly. Don't tell the individual more than is wanted. The accent should be on brevity. After all, the talk has already been given. I've seen a speaker answer 11 questions effectively in one minute and others answer only a few questions in five minutes. If someone asks you to explain a complex principle, for example, aerodynamics or Einstein's theory on relativity, unless you are a master in giving short explanations, simply say, "It would take too long to answer that now, but I'll be happy to discuss it with you after the meeting ends."

6. Verify the listener's satisfaction when it isn't obvious you've answered the question clearly. When the question is more technical, controversial, or complex, ask if you've answered the question to the questioner's satisfaction. There is no need to check with the questioner on simple answers to questions, but check the others. Sometimes the listener can misinterpret the speaker's meaning.

7. Always be ready to corroborate the evidence and data that you include in your answers to questions. The audience may want to know names, dates, places, sources.

8. After acknowledging the question with a nod, a "thank you," or an "um hmm," be sure to look out at the whole audience to answer every question. Don't get locked into a tête-à-tête with the questioner and look only at that person. You're still the speaker, and the audience is still interested in hearing everything you say. They want to feel that you're also talking to them. Looking at one person for too long a time is a sure way to lose the audience in the question and answer period which is the real closing of your speech. Again, acknowledge the question but then look out at the entire audience and answer to all. Of course, you should glance back at the questioner a few times. If an answer takes longer than a few seconds, force yourself to look at the entire audience.

Many good speakers have ruined the occasion by getting into a conversation with just a few members of the audience who continue asking question after question. Keep it moving. Get as many different individuals involved as possible.

9. Treat two questions from the same person, the double-barreled question, as two separate questions. If you treat them as one question your answer could be confusing and probably not complete.

10. Admit you don't have an answer if you really don't have one.

Don't try to beat around the bush or generalize. There's nothing wrong with not having all the answers. Be honest. Or say, "I don't know but I'll find out for you." You'll have to get the person's name and address, however, so that you can get back to him or her. And *do* keep your promise.

11. Be factual and accurate. Too often a quick answer, unsupported by specific evidence, misses the goal completely. Therefore, don't use the following phrases: "They say . . ." or, "A recent report . . ." or, "It is well known . . ." Train yourself to speak in specific, accurate facts and figures. Use names of people when possible and permissible.

12. Rotate the way in which you allow questions to be asked. Let individuals from different sides of the room or auditorium, front, back, and middle, have a chance. Some speakers allow only those in front or on one side to ask questions, and this turns off others who want to be involved. Spread the opportunity to ask questions all around the room in order to maintain the interest of all.

TABOOS FOR QUESTION AND ANSWER SESSIONS

So much for the positive things to do in question and answer sessions. Now let's discuss some dont's, things to avoid that can trap you.

1. Don't grade questions by telling a questioner, "Oh, that's a good question," but not telling all others that theirs are too. Simply answer the question.

2. Don't argue with anyone. State your response and end it there. You only lose ground when you argue.

3. Don't allow one person to keep asking question after question. One or two questions from the same person are enough. Simply say, "Many others have questions. I'll get back to you if there's time." Or, after you've answered the question, look away and acknowledge someone else quickly. Always be friendly.

4. Be careful never to begin your answer to a question with any of the following: "Well, obviously . . . ," "As I said in my talk . . . ," "As I said . . . ," or, "Anyone should know the answer to that . . .". These are all "put down" phrases and may unintentionally insult or embarrass the questioner and the audience. Avoid these and other needling phrases.

5. Don't put your hands on your hips while you are speaking but especially while you are answering questions. This may be interpreted by the audience as talking down to them.

6. Don't point one finger at your audience while you are speaking. It's a scolding pose and preachy. Nobody likes to be talked

down to. Keep a friendly face and a pleasant voice for best results.

HANDLING OBJECTIONS

When I first began giving speeches to clubs and in public I would always fight an objection. I would argue with the person who was objecting to a belief I had expressed or to a fact or statistic I had stated. I always lost on those occasions. Remember these words: "A person convinced against their will, is of the same opinion still." It isn't necessary to argue and, in fact, may do more harm than good. Ever since then I listen to the objection, keep my cool, and simply say, "Thank you for your opinion." Sometimes I add, "This is America. Everybody is entitled to their own convictions." I like what Voltaire said, "I disapprove of what you say, but I will defend to the death your right to say it."

Sometimes some members of an audience just want to give a speech. They want their opinions to be heard, and they have that right. So let them have their say without fighting. Everything will go much smoother and the audience will appreciate it. I'm not suggesting that you compromise beliefs or principles, only that it's necessary to control your emotions and avoid pointless arguments. If some individuals are nasty, unfair, unkind, or even ruthless in their comments, the audience will realize this and may even tell the individual. I've seen this happen frequently. In such an instance, let the audience have their say and then end it by saying, "Thank you for your opinion." You might also add, "But I surely can't agree with it."

There have been times when I've won an audience because I've taken a stand when an objector says, "I don't feel that's true at all," or "I don't believe that." Then, I would be taking a stand based on principle, what I know to be true, or a deep belief. I usually state my point emphatically and intensely but not with undue emotion or rancor. I briefly give the reasons why I disagree with the individual.

HANDLING HECKLERS

Heckling is a different situation altogether from objections. In the dictionary to heckle is defined as "to badger with questions, comments or jibes; to torment, to insult, to harass a person."

Sometimes certain types of individuals purposely want to insult, harass, or thwart the speech or efforts of another person in public. In a humorous talk, if a speaker is confronted by a heckler, the speaker can answer with a funny one-liner. This might also work during a serious talk. For example, when the press corps badgered President Kennedy about appointing his brother Bobby as attorney general, he answered in this way: "I thought the practice would do Bobby some good." It got a big laugh from the members of the press conference and they stopped bothering him about the fact.

In a serious talk, however, it wouldn't be wise to try and keep topping the heckler. This would amount to playing a game of one-upmanship, and the talk and its purpose would get lost in the exchange. Again, keep your cool, check your emotions, and wait until the person stops talking. If the same individual keeps interrupting, the audience will soon take action of some kind that will stop it.

If you think of a clever response, use it, but some hecklers might keep trying to top you. Responding in kind encourages some people, and you want to silence the individual, not provide encouragement. Yet, a little jovial or good-natured heckling is a good thing for any speaker to handle. It offers a change of pace. Some speakers even welcome it.

You'll find books filled with heckler-stoppers, but don't use corny or silly ones to put down a heckler during a serious speech. It will take away from your image and you may lose the respect of the audience.

When sincere questions are asked, even though they may be addressed to you in an irritating way, do answer them as well as you can. Try not to show irritation; it may only bait a heckler. Ignore any questioner who is obviously heckling. You could try using the direct approach, as one speaker I once heard did: "I don't know what I'd without you, but I'd rather!"

The most positive things you can do to prevent heckling are to keep your speaking vital, keep the speech moving, use a change of pace, get the audience involved, use visual aids, and vary your tone. In short, be alive, act alive, talk alive. It's the speaker's responsibility to keep the audience awake and interested. Your enthusiasm will do more to curb interrupters and hecklers than any other technique.

If you encounter a hostile audience, keep your speaking vital, maintain your poise, and try to emphasize the points of agreement you have with the audience. Don't try to shout people down. In fact, you'll have much more success if you lower your voice and speak in a softer manner. Again, dwell on points of agreement in the beginning and then make your own point emphatically and state the areas of disagreement. Also, give your reasons for disagreeing. Do this briefly; don't prolong it. You are there to give your ideas, beliefs, convictions, and principles, not to debate, argue, or fight.

METHODS OF ANTICIPATING QUESTIONS AND OBJECTIONS

Once you have prepared your talk, perhaps with visual aids, you should take time to consider seriously what questions or objections might be brought up after you talk, for then you will have the ammunition—the facts or proof—you need to meet the objections or answer the questions. Usually, you can readily surmise the questions and objections people might raise. Again, preparation is half the battle.

Anticipating objections is the first step. You stand a much better chance of giving a successful speech if you can effectively answer and perhaps overcome objections to your ideas, plans, or proposals. Have slides, charts, or other visual and oral evidence ready to refute or overcome objections. Sometimes you can even turn an objection around and make it work for you. For instance, in one company situation the research department wanted an employee hired to keep up with the requests of all the departments, but the company was objecting because it did not want to add additional personnel to any department at that time even as replacements. The research department responded by saying, "If all departments are cutting back and no personnel will be added in spite of attrition from death, retirement, or turnover, then the departments will need their information earlier than ever. This means we will have to speed up our activities, which means we will need more help." They convinced the company.

Even if you cannot refute or counter an objection, the least you can do is to recognize it. This will show you understand it; just by listening to it and recognizing it you will have taken the emotion out of the situation. But do try to answer it. The more prepared information you have, the more likely you are to succeed. Answer with evidence, which should include the benefits that will happen as a result. Sell benefits, not just facts.

Perhaps the best way to meet objections, where possible, is to use "bottom-line" reasoning: showing the financial gains. It might be costs that can be avoided or profits that will be accumulated. If the benefits are not financial, this rule still applies: *Sell the Benefits to Sell the Plan.*

PREPARING FOR A PRESS CONFERENCE OR A CONGRESSIONAL INQUIRY

First, all the things I've written about anticipating questions and objections after giving your speech apply 100 percent to any kind of meeting with the press or congress. Always be prepared, even with visual aids: charts, photographs, statistics, facts, or testimonies. Visual aids may not always be appropriate, but don't overlook this aspect. There are standard kinds of visual aids that would be appropriate for using in a press conference or congressional inquiry.

Have a statement printed and ready to give to the press. Pack it with the essentials of your side of the case. You're a lot safer with a printed statement well thought out and prepared in advance. You could read a statement and also have ready a handout giving greater detail, defending, or even enhancing your position.

But it's the question and answer sessions that I really want to cover here. A group of TV, radio, newspaper, and magazine reporters could swoop down on you for "a few words and a few answers..." about almost any topic: pollution, crime, unemployment, the OSHA, the EEOC, or you could be subpoenaed by Congress for one of these problems.

A story is told about the senator who came to the "Meet the Press" studio armed with a list of reminders: be candid, and straightforward; appear thoughtful; be modest; give some short answers. All of these reminders are the essence of good preparation, but let's talk specifically about what can happen.

First, some interviewers will obfuscate the issues by using complex words, technical terms, or words that convey a double meaning. Also, many will use jargon or acronyms and confuse listeners. Some examples would be: feedback loop, GAAT, actuarial, certiorari, enzymatic, and so on. Avoid large, uncommon, or ambiguous terms; eliminate jargon, or explain it. Your purpose for speaking to the press or an inquiry should be the same as for speaking to any other audience: to get your ideas across clearly, to clarify facts or state the truth.

Always try to explain statistics and use analogies to make them clearer. Break large sums down. For example, if a proposed new government agency is going to cost $10 million a year to run, break down this cost so that it is comprehensible. The congresswoman talking about it, for example, said, "It will cost every American family just 25¢ a year. If you have brought photographs, make sure they are timely.

Learn to cope with the aggressive and often critical approaches of reporters. Forewarned is forearmed. The reporter's job is to get a good story, and the spicier it is the better. Your job is to give your facts or story clearly and accurately. This takes preparation. It's best to be prepared with 30- to 60-second minispeeches that you can tie in with answers to questions you are asked. The interviewers or reporters are paid for asking questions that will stimulate quotable answers. They want you to talk, but they also want interesting information.

For example, an oil company representative who is prepared with the right kind of answers can do a lot of good, positive image-building for the company. He or she might be asked, "Since the oil industry is in disfavor with the American public over excessive profits, how can you justify those profits?" That is a loaded question that can be anticipated. A prepared answer might be, "Actually, our profits aren't high enough. To meet the government's goal of increased domestic oil production, we need to do much more exploration and we must build more refineries. To do this we'll have to earn much more money."

Other guidelines include:

Keep a positive attitude.
Be yourself.

Tell it like it is.

Don't lose your temper or argue.

Give more than just "yes" and "no" answers.

Explain your stand.

Tell your story as it relates to the public interest.

Don't knock your customers, the buying public.

A few more tips now on better preparation for a press conference or congressional inquiry. Business people are skeptical of the media. Here are some suggestions. If you are sponsoring a conference, large or small, before the press, bring along an articulate and competent spokesperson who knows the answers and can handle the questions expertly. Too many companies allow untrained, unappealing, and even hostile or incompetent individuals to represent them. This just makes a bad situation worse. If you are attending a congressional inquiry, you should have witnesses prepared to explain or answer questions clearly, concisely, and accurately. Honesty and candor create credibility.

Be prompt in arriving and give your spokesperson or witness prepared statements. Here's how. Give them a course or written materials (1) to help them learn the thinking and techniques of the press and congress, (2) to help them learn to control their fear and anxiety and to become more confident and poised under pressure.

Send these key people to a speaking course or organize a practice session for them using videotape so that they can improve their images and their voices. Include information on the use of visual aids to tell your story. Give them each a copy of this book as a beginning. It will pay big dividends for you. The press and congress needs facts; the public wants to know, and reporters are the eyes and ears of the public. The press will want to talk with a company representative. Look on the press in a positive way, and don't think of them or treat them as adversaries or as a nuisance. Provide background briefings for the press corps. Try to meet their deadlines.

Television is a powerful, visual medium. Use it. Most stations are enlarging their evening newscasts to two hours and have staffs of journalists. There's great opportunity here for all sides to air their views. Two key people on TV news staffs are: the assignment editor and the news director. Contact local stations; seek out news people. Hold a cocktail party for the press to get to know them and to let them get to know you, your company, or organization. Hold such a conference when you have positive news to report. Establish a rapport with the press to assure a positive image with the public and perhaps more objective coverage when trouble strikes.

CHAPTER 8

Humorous Speaking Made Easy

HOW AND WHEN TO USE HUMOR

"Men and women will confess to treason, arson, murder, false teeth, or a wig, but how many will own up to a lack of humor?" If that observation by Frank Moore Colby was true when he expressed it in the early 1900s, it's even more accurate in our fast-moving, complex, changing world today. We need humor even more now as a release from tension, stress, and problems. Nobody wants to confess to lacking a sense of humor, yet few people use it, and few speakers use humor in their speeches to relate to people and help make their points.

In the past in speech courses instructors warned, "Use humor sparingly, make it relevant, and keep it short." Times have changed, and there appears today to be a greater need for using more humor to relate to audiences. However, it should always be relevant to your topic and help make your point. And brevity is still the soul of wit.

Humor should be used whenever you have appropriate material or anecdotes that will help make your point, hold the attention of your audience, or entertain them. It's more difficult to keep audiences attentive today in our visual society. Humor adds a key quality to public speaking or, for that matter, in communication anytime.

The difficulty with using humor arises in two ways: (1) where to find worthwhile material and (2) how to tell jokes effectively. I will say a lot about both problems throughout this chapter.

In the past I would say to executives to whom I was teaching public speaking, "Don't feel you have to be humorous. Listeners respond just as eagerly to logic, emotion, sincerity, honesty, vitality, and humility. But humor helps and the audience always appreciates it as a change of pace. Yet, humor is not essential and sometimes it isn't even appropriate." This is basically still true, but I will adapt it by saying that although humor is not essential, it is more welcome, more appreciated, and more necessary for audience interest today. After all, speakers are competing with top comedians and writers whose humor comes into our living rooms on TV day and night. Situation comedies are prominent in the top TV favorites; books and cassettes on humor are flourishing; and 40 percent of the top 100 TV commercials have humor in them. All these trends reflect a greater need and acceptance of humor today.

I've even found that humor can be appropriate in a eulogy, especially if the deceased was in some way tied in with the entertainment world. For example, Danny Thomas delivered the eulogy for Frank Sinatra's mother following her tragic death. The eulogy, delivered in a church in California, was filled with quotations of Mrs. Sinatra about her son. They were beautiful, human thoughts and brought release and laughter in a sad atmosphere. However, too many speakers aren't effective in using humor from a platform or in front of an audience anywhere.

Consider the speaker who had been serious for 15 minutes of her speech but suddenly said to the audience, "I'm going to tell a joke." The listeners found this funny and laughed hard. Then she told the joke and nobody laughed. She was too serious. The audience tends to reflect the speaker's mood, movements, and facial expressions, so one important rule for speakers is: Don't be too serious. And don't expect laughs if you have a somber, sober, stoic appearance and a harsh voice. Lighten up. A smile can put an audience at ease and lead them to expect a good time. A smile is a sign of confidence and a reflection of friendliness.

It is not good to laugh at your own jokes. I've seen speakers laugh at their jokes but the audience doesn't laugh. Phyllis Diller has a wild laugh that makes the audience laugh even if the joke doesn't draw a response, but that's an exception.

Sometimes jokes will not be successful. What should you do? Well, if you don't have a hearty, funny laugh like Phyllis Diller, be ready with a back-up joke or move quickly to your next sentence. Don't look or act stunned and dumbfounded. Keep your speech moving. Your vitality might just save the situation. A back-up comment or another quick joke has often saved comedians and speakers. Don't think that ad-libs are always spontaneous. More often they were prepared ahead for just such a situation.

Occasionally, when a funny line or story doesn't get a laugh from the audience, I'll react with something like this: "I just threw that in; I should have thrown it out." Usually I'll get a laugh from this. Some speakers simply move on to another gag or anecdote and hope it gets a laugh.

Most comedians and many speakers try their stories and jokes out on friends or acquaintances first or on a small, informal group. If it goes over with them, it's worth trying with a large audience. Also, it's important to find good jokes or one-liners, and that I'll cover later in this chapter.

Practice and experience are just as important to effective joke-telling as they are for any skill, but the art of telling jokes is even more challenging than the art of serious speaking. The reason for this is that it takes a greater skill to artfully tell humorous stories and it usually is harder to get laughs than to inform or inspire listeners.

You are probably wondering how to develop the art of telling funny stories or of making people laugh. The answer is that the skill comes from doing. Start looking for humor; you'll find it everywhere. Then start using the jokes and stories you find on friends and at informal gatherings or wherever anyone will listen to you. Try them out on your doctor, hairdresser, druggist, grocer, or neighbor.

You can also tape-record your humor and then critique it for brevity, spirit, pauses or lack of them, emphasis or lack of it, and pace. It's important that you think the story is funny or don't use it.

Make sure your speech is clear. Check your pronunciation and enunciation. Pay close attention to your timing when you are giving the punch line. Do pause long enough before saying the punch line and do say it clearly and emphatically. You will know if you have done it well when people laugh at what you say. That's why an audience of one anytime, even when you are taping, is a big help in trying to improve your delivery.

Get into the habit of exchanging jokes with others. Ask them if they've heard any good ones lately and write them down. But, always remember to practice. Tell friends you talk with on the phone the newest joke you've heard or a funny experience you've had. Tell them and see if they laugh. If you use the ones that are the funniest, they'll soon be a part of you and unforgettable. And you'll develop a knack for telling them in the best way.

Once again, your main purpose is to get your point across. Humor can help you accomplish this if you make your stories relevant to the subject. Don't just throw in gags or funny sayings to be humorous or clever. Relevancy is a major criterion for supporting evidence of any kind. Your humor should support your topic, theme, or point. Of course, a key requirement of a joke is that it be funny.

The best rule for not embarrassing your listeners and not offending anyone is this: don't use off-color stories, insulting ethnic gags, or remarks about religion. Remember former Secretary of Agriculture, Earl Butz, who got into hot water by telling a religious joke to an audience. He received complaints from religious people everywhere and even the Vatican. Later, on another occasion Butz told one person a nasty ethnic expression. This person then quoted Butz in a book he published and Butz was asked by the president to resign. Just as with profanity, you will always offend people in your audience by using off-color jokes or ethnic or religious stories that are intended to insult.

Keep your jokes and stories short and to the point. Don't use shaggy dog stories from the platform. It would have to be exceptional to be included in the talk. Emulate the king of one-liners, Henny Youngman. Now in his seventies, according to *People* magazine those one-liners earn him more than $330,000 a year. His stories are rarely longer than a sentence or two. His newest booklet, "Super One-Liners," contains 1008 one-liners. One example is, "My car is like a baby; it won't go anywhere without a rattle."

Bob Hope is another master of the one-liner. The key to his success on TV and in stage shows is the same now as when he first went on radio: topical humor and brevity. The more current and topical his gags are, the more laughs he gets. Of course, he has a stable of top writers, but the point here is that topical humor based on the news of the day will be successful with any audience. Looking at it another way, topical humor is relevant to our daily lives.

Although the anecdote has declined in popularity for use in speeches, there are some perfect ones that can help you make your point, get a rapport, or entertain. If it gets laughs and fits the talk, use it. The secret is to link the point of the anecdote to the point of your speech.

HOW NOT TO USE HUMOR

In a fortune cookie I opened recently after a Chinese dinner, I discovered a good rule for speakers. The fortune said, "Wit and humor at another's expense cannot be." This is good advice. Don't poke fun at others. You will alienate individuals and antagonize the entire audience. Poke fun at yourself instead. Never apologize, but give the members of your audience a laugh on you.

Kenneth McFarland says as he begins, "I guess you expected a younger man." (McFarland is tall, handsome, and bald.) He then says, "Well, I want you to know I used to have hair. I had a crew cut, but the crew bailed out!" And the truth brings a big laugh. The laugh is at his own expense, not at the expense of his listeners.

Don't tell your audience that you're going to tell a joke. Just do it. Explaining what you're going to do is boring and takes away from the story.

Don't use material that makes fun of classes or types of people, particularly individuals with handicaps of a physical nature.

Don't use a dialect unless it's an authentic reproduction. They are fine to use if you're really good at it.

Don't hurry on to another joke while the audience is still laughing or applauding. Relax, wait, give them time to enjoy the joke. Hurry when the joke dies, not when it goes over well.

Don't try to fit in a joke that has nothing to do with your talk or the audience. Find appropriate and suitable stories that help you make your points.

Don't ever read a joke.

TECHNIQUES OF TOP COMEDIANS AND PROFESSIONAL SPEAKERS

When it comes to recalling jokes, most people need help. Almost every day I hear someone say, "I just can't remember jokes," or, "I can recall the joke but I forget the punch line." This is normal. Joke-telling is an art. However, some jokes and puns are so bad it's better to forget them.

Memorizing short jokes and anecdotes is fine, but trying to memorize longer stories word for word is deadly unless you're an expert. Besides, you will lose your spontaneity and sound canned and formal if you memorize longer stories.

Study the techniques and styles of the professionals: Milton Berle, Danny Thomas, Alan King, Henny Youngman, Bob Hope. They are natural, brief, and their jokes are to the point. They don't drag out a story or include boring, unnecessary details. Listen to these professionals in person or buy their tapes and records. Time their jokes. Note their spirit, pauses, emphasis, and clarity. Then go do likewise.

When you study the techniques of the top stand-up comedians, you'll discover that they have a number of things in common with top speakers (who use a lot of humor), such as Dr. Herb True, Cavett Robert, Dr. Kenneth McFarland, Bill Gove, Larry Wilson, and others. First, they have an organized system of remembering. Usually, they remember key words and categories, which are all they need.

Once Henny Youngman appeared on a TV variety show emceed by

Pat Boone. Boone took out the Yellow Pages and challenged Youngman to come up with a gag for every category mentioned. Youngman complied and didn't hesitate once. You can do this too if you learn to remember the key words of a joke and learn them by categories.

Some common categories to work on are: marriage, wife, husband, politics, doctors, sports, movies, space. Sometimes key words of jokes are also categories: Las Vegas, gambling, parking, driving, Wall Street.

Master the joke or story by telling it every day to people. Learn to recall the story by categorizing it and picking out the key words. Youngman ties the two techniques together and says, "I have five brothers-in-law. None have done well. First brother-in-law: I wish he'd get a job so I'd know what kind of work he's out of. Second brother-in-law: a genius, opened a tall man's shop in Tokyo. Third brother-in-law: tells people he's a diamond-cutter but mows the lawn at Yankee stadium." Well, you get the idea. See how easy it is? I recalled those jokes from memory because I used the category and key word method (category—brother-in-law; key words—work, Tokyo, diamond, or baseball).

Another common trait of top joke-tellers is their ability to be brief. Although Myron Cohen, Danny Thomas, and Alan King often tell longer stories, these stories are really short when they are compared to the ones nonprofessionals tell. Practicing by telling the stories over and over will give you the ability to be brief.

Organization is also essential for speaking or telling jokes. It's the key to remembering jokes. Writing them down when you hear them is the first step towards learning them. Telling them frequently until you've learned them is the next step. But to assure instant recall do what the professionals do: mentally file the jokes in categories and pick out the key words that will remind you of the essence of them and their punch lines.

I was once introduced to Milton Berle as a speech consultant. Before he even greeted me he asked me, "Did you hear about the man with the speech inpediment?" I said, "No." Berle then said, "He had one arm shorter than the other!" You see, as soon as Berle heard the key word "speech" when I was introduced to him, he thought of the joke and told it. Notice also that it was concise.

One time I watched Henny Youngman on stage in Chicago. He had told about 50 one-liners and some 2- or 3-line stories. He had told so many jokes that he began to draw a blank. But all performers have blanks occasionally. Youngman walked to the side of the stage and spoke to some people at a ringside table. Still he appeared not to think of a joke. Then, he happened to ask them, "Are you comfortable?" They said "Yes!" And at that moment, upon hearing the key word "comfortable," he moved back to the middle of the stage and told a joke.

He did as I expected. Told about the man hit by a car. The policeman sat the man against a wall, put a blanket around him and asked, "Are you comfortable?" The man replied, "I make a good living!"

If you tell professionals a punch line often they can tell you the joke. If you learn the punch line, you can usually think of the details, but put the jokes in your own words. Let's practice now with a few examples. I'll provide a couple of jokes. You should try to list the key words that would help you recall the jokes. Write down what you feel are the best words to remember it instantly.

A fellow asks his girlfriend's father permission to marry his daughter. The father asks him, "Can you support a family?" The fellow says, "Yes." The father then shouts: "Good! There are seven of us!"

What would you pick as the key words for this joke? I would choose "marriage," "support," and "seven kids."

Try another one.

Two women are talking. The first one says, "I understand your husband drowned and left you $2 million. Can you imagine, $2 million, and he couldn't read or write!" The second woman replies, "Yes. And he couldn't swim either!"

I would choose as key words or categories the following: for categories—money, husband, inheritance, death; for key words—money, drowning, read, write, swim.

Think of wit as well as humor when you are trying to win an audience. The late Pope John won over the press corps of the world at his first press conference. A reporter inquired, "Your Excellency, how many people work here at theVatican?" Pope John, with a twinkle in his eye, replied instantly, "About half of them!" The press roared with laughter, and Pope John had won their respect.

But remember these words about wit by William Hazlitt, the English essayist, "Wit is the salt of the conversation, not the food."

THE BEST KINDS OF HUMOR

Someone has observed that everything is funny as long as it happens to someone else. For some odd reason a person finds it funny to see someone else slip on a banana peel and fall, but that same person finds it embarrassing when it happens to her or him. So remember to poke fun at yourself, not at your listeners.

Humor is always at its best when you put it in your own words, with your own style and personality. Use your own pace, timing, and emphasis. Don't try to copy anyone else's style of speaking or joke-telling. Make it your own. Also personalize your stories and anecdotes.

Change the names of any characters to the name of someone relevant to the occasion (or the name of someone in the audience). This has much greater appeal than stories that use names of unknown people.

Frank Hardesty, a professional teacher and speaker, does this with all of his stories. For example, if the individual in charge of the program is named Jack Hall, Frank might say, "Jack Hall has two rules to guide his management: first, Jack Hall is always right; second, if Jack Hall isn't right, revert back to rule number one!" This is a short, funny, personalized joke that gets loads of laughter whether it's true or not.

I have heard the same joke told by five different comedians, but the joke sounds different each time because each comedian puts it in his or her own words and style. Any good joke will get a laugh if it is told well. But don't tell it in someone else's style. This is especially true of longer jokes, stories, or anecdotes. And don't use someone else's personal story or experience unless you give credit to that person. Even then, the audience may not laugh if they've heard the story. Try to get fresh material or to put a new twist or slant to older stories.

Remember that humor is best in brief form. So build a collection of one, two, and three-liners—jokes that make a point. I like to use the one about the woman who asks a police officer, "Can I park here?" The police officer says, "No!" "But why not?" she asks, "How about these other people who have parked their cars here?" The police officer tells her, "They didn't ask!"

I personally believe that the best kind of humor is whatever fits the occasion, fits the audience, or clinches a point or idea, but I also feel that the best kind is whatever makes people laugh. My collection of puns, jokes, poems, anecdotes, stories, limericks, bloopers, and one-liners are kept in an "active" file because they work for me and are the ones that get me laughs anywhere, anytime.

I've made a study of comedians since I was in my early teens. I've noted that the the top professionals will keep the good stories and laughs in frequent use for decades of entertaining. Henny Youngman is still using some of the best material he used the first time I heard him in person a few decades ago. They are still hilarious in spite of their age or the number of times they've been repeated, so keep the good ones you hear in an active file for ready use anytime.

I once said to a comedian who still uses a lot of his old material: "You sure have adult humor. All your jokes are over 21 years old." The group with us laughed, but the comedian didn't. It was all in fun, but there was too much truth in it. So be considerate.

The first objective—and maybe the only one—of a joke of any kind is that it makes people laugh. It won't make any point at all if it's not funny.

Remember that audiences love topical humor, jokes on current topics: TV shows and personalities, movies, books, politics, songs, advertisements, fads, magazines, anything in the newspapers that day.

Short poems sometimes can be used easily to make a point humorously, for instance, "He finally got his hair trimmed; but it wasn't dad or mom; it seems another fellow, asked him to the senior prom!"

For many years I gave a talk about actual bloopers "on the air." (A blooper is an unintended spoonerism, any mistake, or a mispronunciation that is funny.) It was an after-dinner speech and went over so well that I've always included a couple of planned bloopers in all my talks. Audiences love the mistakes of others.

Some examples of bloopers follow.

Hollywood reporter: "It's rumored that the former movie starlet is expecting her fifth child in a month."

Political speech: "If I'm elected, I can promise you the finest local government money can buy."

Radio commercial: "Men, when it's time to shave, you have a date with our two-headed model."

Another radio commercial: "Folks, don't forget to shop this weekend at your A and Poo Feed Store."

A newspaper ad: "Johnson's Department store offers these special large-size bathing suits for ladies at give-away prices. Now's the time to buy a bathing suit for a ridiculous figure."

You get the idea. When you hear one, write it down.

WHERE TO FIND HUMOR

The general answer to where to find humor is "everywhere." Specifically here's a list of the usual sources.

1. Start looking in your own home. Get into the habit of clipping out joke columns from newspapers, magazines, and advertisements. Keep a pen or pencil and pad handy near the TV, radio, and telephone so that everytime you hear a good story, one that you feel you can use, you can write it down. Even the mistakes of personalities you hear or see can be humorous material. Of course, you can also tape-record the work of, comedians you see and hear on TV and radio. Johnny Carson's nightly monologue, Bob Hope's stand-up jokes, and the jokes of many comedians on TV talk and variety shows offer good sources for humorous material. This costs nothing and you will have the best writers and performers working for you. And don't overlook humor you can find in books from your own home library.

2. Local libraries often have shelves of books on humor, jokes, the art of humor. They may also have a thesaurus of humor or a book that is a treasury of humor. Again, it costs nothing to use these. You can even research jokes on a certain topic.

3. Some bookstores have a section on wit and humor. There are many paperbacks that are filled with jokes, which are cheaper than hardcover books. And don't overlook the local drugstore for paperbacks on humor.

4. Record stores have albums on humor: George Carlin, Bill Cosby, Henny Youngman, and many others. Some are available also on cassettes.

5. General Cassette Corporation has the largest catalog listing of cassettes that contain jokes from all over the world. You can have the masters' voices and styles entertaining you in your own living room, and you'll learn from them. Write to: General Cassette Corporation, 1324 22nd Avenue, Box 6940, Phoenix, Arizona 85005.

6. See comedians and top professional speakers in person anytime you can. Keep a notebook and pen handy. Go to supper clubs and hotels, banquets and conventions, rallies and sales conventions. You'll get more material than you know what to do with.

7. Carry 3 × 5 cards or a notebook with you everywhere. At meetings, luncheons, and dinners, anywhere you are with people, write down the quips, witty remarks, jokes, and funny lines that you hear. Neil Simon, the great comedy writer, says that he gets most of his ideas by listening to the funny things people say in everyday conversations. It's a rich source. Some years ago, Phyllis Diller paid homemakers $5 for each funny family incident, expression, or experience they wrote to her.

8. Get an annual subscription to *Orben's Current Comedy*, a primary source of humor for speakers, comedians, salespeople, and executives. It's a four-page newsletter that comes out 24 times a year. Write for a catalog and costs and try the three-month trial subscription (Orben's Comedy Center, 700 Orange St., Wilmington, Delaware 19801).

9. Use your imagination to think up funny sayings or comments on the topics of the day. In other words, don't sell yourself short as a creator of comedy. Try writing some funny lines yourself. You'll come up with some good ones if you work at it. And who knows, in time, you could publish your own comedy newsletter.

10. If you're seriously interested in public speaking, join the National Speakers Association, an organization of professional and non-professional speakers. They have a national convention annually, during which you'll hear the best professional speakers. Each year a dozen new speakers also are given the chance to talk to the convention. Write for information to: National Speakers Association, P.O. Box 6296, Phoenix, Arizona 85005.

Finally, here is a list of suggested books—and one record—available in many bookstores. I have them and find them to be worthwhile. Look through them before you buy them.

The Public Speaker's Handbook of Humor, Larry Eisenberg, Association Press, New York, 1967.

Handbook of Humor for All Occasions, Jacob Braude, Prentice-Hall, Inc., Englewood Cliffs, New Jersey, 1959.

10,000 Jokes, Toasts and Stories, Lewis Copeland, Garden City Books, Garden City, New York, 1940.

Treasury of Modern Humor, Martha Lupton, Maxwell Droke, Indianapolis, Indiana, 1938.

Speaker's Desk Book, Martha Lupton, Grosset & Dunlap, Inc., New York, 1948.

Any of Henny Youngman's many paperbacks. They're all loaded with jokes on every topic and they're all brief.

Finally, Henny Youngman's record "The Best of the Worst of Henny Youngman," 1973, is a classic.

TYING ANECDOTES INTO YOUR OBJECTIVE OR TOPIC

We've already noted that humor should be related to your topic or be relevant to the purpose, point, or objective of your talk. But sometimes you will want to use a topical bit of humor that may not be related. You can use it if you consider tying the joke or witty remark into your topic.

Listen closely to Johnny Carson's monologue at the start of "The Tonight Show." Note how he makes a half-dozen topics of the day all tie in together. He does it by using clever transitions to give a connection or a link to everything he says. This is the mark of a professional speaker or entertainer. These are planned ahead carefully. Even the lines following "groaners," jokes that make the audience groan, are anticipated, such as "Oh, a hostile audience tonight." Even when a joke gets a good laugh Carson usually knows ahead that it will and he has a remark prepared, such as, "Well, I can do no harm tonight. When I pass through the audience you can touch the hem of my jacket." But the true transitions between laughs are what tie-in the jokes and quips with his theme, "the happenings of the day."

Other transitions follow.

"Well, what's new today?" This makes a fine transition from regular news of the day to keep a fluency to the patter.

Continuing,

I've noted the new TV commercials for Right Guard Deodorant. But there's a newer deodorant just out. It's not a stick, not a pad, not a spray. It's a shower!"

The twist is the "shower."

Here is another transition:

"Let's see, what else is new? Oh, for the Ed McMahon's and the Dean Martin's here's a new sure-cure for hangovers. Go up to the suffering man, shake his hand, and say, 'That sure was a beautiful girl you married last night!' "

Here's still another transition:

"Americans love new things, anything new—toothpastes, breakfast cereals, toys, cars."

Now here's a joke:

"The reason so many people buy new automobiles is because they have to pay cash when they are riding on a bus."

Remember, I was not trying to provide excellent jokes, but rather I was trying to illustrate the value of transitional phrases to make them fit your talk.

CHAPTER 9

Professional Tips for Speaking or Being Interviewed on TV, Film, or Radio

DO'S AND DON'T'S OF USING A MICROPHONE

When I was a youngster there weren't microphones to practice with. Now, just about every home has a tape recorder with a microphone, so it's easy for you to practice and become accustomed to and unafraid of handling a "live" microphone (or "mike").

My first suggestion on the Do side of the list is to use a tape recorder right now if you have one and put the microphone in front of you. If you have a small holder or a stand for the microphone, so much the better. Put it right in front of you so that you can learn as you read about it.

Whenever you're going to give a speech or report into a microphone, check it before you give your speech. The best time to check equipment is before the event begins. It's too late once everyone is present, and it's not professional to tamper with microphones or other equipment once a program has started.

Check to see if you can easily adjust the microphone to your height. Set it so that it comes up to your chin. Then it will not block your face, and you can look out over it. Check to see if it has an on-off switch. See that it's "on" when you start. Then, be careful never to touch the mike again if it's a standing one. Many speakers have begun talking into a "dead" microphone, and others have handled the stand or mike and accidently turned it off.

Next, check to see if there's a volume control. Have someone set it for you as you practice speaking into the microphone. Nothing annoys an audience faster than a shrill voice coming through an amplifier exploding with distortion. Overmodulation causes distortion, static, and broken eardrums. If there's an engineer handling the controls of the speaker system, you'll have no problem.

Another good preparation to assure the proper volume is to have someone stand in the rear of the auditorium or in the back of a smaller room as you practice. They can tell you when the volume is set just right for your voice and projection.

It's best to keep the microphone 4 to 6 inches away from your face. Sometimes it's necessary to bring the mike closer, as it may not pick up your voice well beyond a few inches. Again, keep the mike at or just about chin level. Always turn the mike at a right angle instead of pointing it directly towards your face and mouth. This will enable you to talk across the front of the microphone rather than directly into it and will prevent you from popping your p's, b's, d's, and other exploding letters. You will cause a popping and even distortion by talking directly into the mike.

Do speak up. Too many speakers expect the mike to do all the work. A microphone cannot provide emphasis. The speaker must put personality into the speaker system and provide the sparkle and vocal variety that make the words come alive. Practice on your tape recorder at home. Have family members or friends evaluate your recordings.

The list of Don'ts begins with: don't touch the mike once you begin your speech. Don't even hang onto the microphone stand or the microphone wire. Put nothing in your hands unless you're exhibiting an article, object, or other type of visual aid. Some microphones are so sensitive that you will cause static and distortion merely by touching the mike.

Don't shout when you are standing just a few inches away from the microphone. Step back when you speak louder or when you shout. Some speakers have blown out the microphone with a sudden, intense shout directly into the mike at close range.

When you are going to speak softly or whisper, step closer to the microphone so you'll be easily heard. And don't let the microphone block your face. Make sure it's at chin level, and placed obliquely to your face.

Once you've started, don't worry about the mike. Think only of your audience and of getting your message across to them. If you keep your voice alive and keep projecting with emphasis, the microphone will work beautifully.

To put it another way, don't expect the mike to do all the work. You must supply the color, the tone, the change of pitch, pace, and emphasis. Make your key words—verbs and adjectives—*Live*!

Occasionally you'll be confronted by a different type of microphone such as a lavalier. This type of microphone is hung around your neck and rests on your chest about 2 or 3 inches under your chin. Often another person will put it on for you. It takes just a second, but often a nervous speaker can't get it on, so let someone else do it for you.

Frequently I am provided with a cordless microphone. This is a small power pack unit with an on-off switch on it. The power pack is a little larger than a cigarette pack and much heavier. It is hung on your belt. The cord to the mike comes up under a jacket or top and the mike pins to your lapel or collar or tie. This particular microphone is about one-third the size of my little finger, round, and just as light. Many stage and TV performers wear them.

I prefer a cordless microphone to a lavalier, mainly because the wire is eliminated. It's easy to trip over the microphone wire when you're wearing it. Also, sometimes I've started walking and almost choked myself when I took one step too far and the wire pulled me back. Watch your movements when you have the mike cord extending from around your neck.

Some speakers like to hold the microphone and carry it around as they speak. I've done this, but I feel that it curbs the gestures of the speaker. It's necessary to have your hands empty and free to communicate. Yet, some speakers want to hold on to something for security. Try to put the microphone in a position other than in your hand throughout your talk.

HOW TO PREPARE FOR FILM OR TV

In the early 1950s when TV first made an impact in the United States, a few schools for TV performing sprang up in most cities. These schools charged a great deal of money to prepare people to work on TV as performers or to be a guest, contestant, or speaker. At that time I had been working for years in radio and hadn't started doing television yet. My colleagues and I laughed and said it was ridiculous to have a school to prepare people to be on TV because all that was necessary was to be yourself. Most of these schools failed. Radio schools, which still abound, teach how to read commercials and news and how to interview. TV schools couldn't add much, so all but a few failed. Those that still operate teach commercial reading or acting. Some also teach news commentary.

When television arrived, performers who had been doing radio for years converted immediately to television without a day of schooling. They had to learn to be under lights, to be aware of which camera was on, and to dress properly for the role they played. In fact, many TV stations in smaller communities had only one camera, so it was easy for the performer to read or speak to just one camera with the red "on" light on top of the camera.

Working on radio was good preparation for TV, but there really was very little to do to prepare for a TV appearance as a speaker, as a guest on an interview program, as a person being interviewed by the press, or as a constestant.

Today, the professional at the local TV station or the network will give you a few necessary pointers for dressing, speaking, and answering questions, but let's go over these basic rules.

First, men should shave as late as possible before their TV appearance, since beards do show up darker. However, you'll almost always be prepared by a makeup artist before going on, and makeup will cover your beard quite well. Take an electric razor with you to the studio. Often, delays will keep you waiting and before you know it you will have a "five o'clock shadow."

Remember, you *are* the visual aid when you're speaking, so neatness in appearance counts. Wear shoes, and a suit or a dress that are most comfortable for you. Wear the colors you feel are best for you. Notice what the TV newspeople and other performers, interviewers, and interviewees wear. You'll see all colors and every style. I've never yet bought a shirt, tie, or suit just for TV. Some ties are too loud or busy, such as floral patterns or small but brightly colored designs.

Perhaps the real preparation for making a film or appearing on TV is getting ready to have something to say and then saying it naturally, clearly, and sincerely. Everything I've written already about preparing a speech or answering questions applies to making a speech or giving a report or commentary on TV. First, limit your topic, as the time you'll be allowed will be strictly enforced. If you're allowed five minutes, that's all you'll have. If it's a live presentation, you'll be cut off before you finish if you go overtime. If you're being filmed or taped and you are running overtime, you'll either be edited later or asked to stop and prepare to cut something in order to finish in the allowed time. The best way to avoid these problems is to time your speech with a stopwatch before you ever get to the studio and make sure you're undertime, not over the allowed time.

The same rules apply for getting a rapport and opening your speech that apply to giving any speech in public. You want to take hold of the attention of your listeners. Since with TV you're also being seen and judged on your looks, try to show a genuine, natural smile. If you're well prepared, the naturalness will usually come through. Because of the hot lights, the tension, and the pressure, most people forget to smile when they speak on TV. Remind yourself to smile.

It helps if you begin with a humorous anecdote or experience or perhaps a clever, witty one-liner or quotation. Select illustrations that are concise. When you're on TV, time is precious. It is necessary to make your point in a short time with few examples, so pick only the best evidence. Make your statements in short sentences and stick to just one topic and just one specific objective.

Use simple language. Avoid using four- and five-syllable words. Spend time finding just the right word—adjective or verb. Every word counts when you have just a few minutes to make your point.

Always have a prepared closing and stick to it. Don't change it. Make it a strong, concise, clear summary of your speech. End with intensity and finality. Be emphatic but not loud. Read Chapter 3 again to find some classic openings and closings. Find a fitting, short poem or quotation to highlight your point or use the summary or call-to-action closing. Be yourself at your best: put your best voice, best face, best thoughts, and best personality forward. Don't be too expressive or assertive, as this is not effective on TV. The camera magnifies large gestures so they will become even more flagrant. Don't use quick or sweeping gestures. But move so you will not appear too formal or frozen.

Be yourself but be conversational. Speak up to show vitality and vocal variety. Don't let your voice be monotonous or colorless. However, on TV it's proper to soften your projection somewhat and modulate your voice more as you speak. It's not necessary to use the power needed before a large audience when you're on a platform. Still, it's necessary to show your emotion and be emphatic to make a point and to transfer conviction to others. Vitality of voice, posture, and spirit are necessary to keep the viewer's interest.

Posture communicates whether you are seated or standing. The camera magnifies posture as well as gestures. If you are seated, sit naturally but erectly in the chair. If you are standing also stand erectly. Slouchy posture gives an appearance of laziness and an impression of sloppiness.

Sometimes TV stations have swivel chairs. Most stations have banished them, however, because guests as well as performers would twist and turn back and forth continuously out of nervousness. Although they were unaware of these movements they annoyed the viewers. Anything that doesn't add, detracts. It's best not to do things that will distract your audience from your message.

PERFECTING YOUR LANGUAGE

Language, whether it's written or spoken, enables us to inform, influence, or entertain others. When we speak, we're never just saying a few words; we're always revealing a human personality, so be careful not to use offending jokes, irritating ethnic phrases, jargon many may not understand, off-color stories, or profanity of any kind. It's even risky to use slang. Any of these may turn off some members of your audience.

When you are preparing your speech for TV write it and then revise it. Prefer concrete, specific words to the general, abstract words. Once you've limited your topic to one dominant purpose or objective, selected specific material suited solely to that purpose, and arranged the material in a definite order and outline, you are ready to concentrate on your choice of words. Now is the time to write and revise, improving on your language, making every word and phrase count towards expressing yourself clearly, convincingly, and colorfully.

As with giving speeches, avoid relying on notes; they will come between you and your audience. It's preferable to commit your outline to memory or perhaps have a large file card with your outline and key ideas printed in large letters resting on a table in front of you or at your side. Memorize the sequence of ideas rather than the words themselves. Speak the ideas spontaneously. Keep the card out of your hands.

I cannot overestimate the importance of words. They are your material; they are your means of transporting ideas. By reading the great books and current newspapers and magazines you will find it easier to choose appropriate words. Reading is one of the best and cheapest ways of keeping abreast of what's going on. Reading will help you broaden your understanding. It will also help you to increase your vocabulary.

Reading one or two newspapers and magazines each day will help you stay informed in all the key areas of life: government, literature, education, management, religion, and entertainment. And if you want to be effective in public speaking you will have to be aware of current news.

When you read, underline or make note of new words or unfamiliar words, and make it a point to look them up in the dictionary. Study them until you know them. This habit will enrich your vocabulary while improving your understanding and communication ability.

All that I have said can be reduced to five words: limit, select, arrange, write, and read. The most important of these for TV, film, or radio is limit.

TELLTALE TRAITS OF AN AMATEUR

Most people do not want to be immature or amateurish in their speaking or writing, at work, on TV, radio, or in films or videotape. Not wanting to be tagged an amateur is the first step towards not being one. Oliver Wendell Holmes summed it up this way: "Success is the result of our mental attitude. And the right mental attitude will bring success in everything you do." Having an attitude of vitality and fluency will motivate you to prepare harder. It's difficult to be fluent under normal conditions of speaking to a group. On TV when you're under hot lights and the signal is given to begin, it's even more difficult.

Have someone critique your appearance before you head for the studio and before you walk out to the cameras and microphone. Even practice sitting in a chair. See how you look with your legs crossed. Amateurs either freeze and stay formal and tacit in a TV interview or they move continually in their chair from sheer nervousness. Try to be natural, not a nervous wreck; at ease, not stiff.

Amateurs don't listen well and usually keep asking, "What did you say?" Poor listeners usually interrupt harshly. There is a tactful way to interrupt, but interrupting is not good communication unless it's to clarify something that has been said.

The most telltale signs of frightened, unprepared speakers or interviewees on TV is body language: folded arms show tension or defensiveness; slouchy posture communicates a dull, listless attitude; weak gestures communicate a lack of conviction; hands around the mouth communicate insecurity.

Slow responses and listless speech reveal poor preparation and often a lack of knowledge or a poor vocabulary. Freud once said, "Even when a person dosen't speak, betrayal oozes out of every pore." Our body language and demeanor speak more loudly than words.

METHODS FOR PRACTICING

An amateur is unskilled and unprepared, so preparation is the first step toward not being amateurish. Preparation breeds confidence. Anything well prepared is already nine tenths accomplished. Analyzing yourself in a mirror as you rehearse a talk or commentary while sitting down or standing up is a good exercise.

It would be ideal if everyone could be videotaped in a studio as they practice. Then they would readily see the telltale faults mentioned previously. The majority of facial tics, poor posture, or irritating mannerisms can be eliminated quickly once an individual sees them. Awareness brings about improvement faster.

Listening to yourself on a tape recorder will help you eliminate the amateurish "ah's" "uh's" "you know's" "Very, very's" "O.K.'s" and other word-whiskers that take away from the clarity of your message.

And finding one person to listen to you and provide an instant evaluation of what you do well and what you can do to improve your content, delivery, and appearance will be excellent preparation. Since most TV and radio appearances are brief, you can quickly go over your talk again and again and commit the outline to memory.

CHAPTER

How to Speak Successfully on Special Occasions

HOW TO PRESENT AN AWARD

Brevity, specificity, simplicity, warmth, spirit, and using human interest data are my key suggestions for giving speeches of introduction, presenting or receiving awards, and to some extent giving reports. All of these qualities mentioned are ideal for giving eulogies as well except that the spirit should be subdued. Let's look at them one at a time.

Always think out and if possible, write out brief ideas about presenting an award. Always mention the person, club, or organization providing the award but put the spotlight on the person receiving the award rather than on the award itself.

Place heavy emphasis on the qualities that enabled the recipient to earn or win the award. Try to include some insight into the individual, a human interest fact, experience, or anecdote but always keep it specific and concise, as well as spirited. It's best to keep your remarks limited to around two or three minutes for most awards, a little longer for an extraordinary award. Also emphasize the pride and pleasure of the sponsor of the award.

HOW TO RECEIVE AN AWARD OR A GIFT

It should always be a happy occasion to receive an award, especially an award or reward at a retirement party. So the first suggestion for accepting an award is to be happy about it. Show your true feelings of pride. Allow your emotions to come through. Put a smile on your face and be joyful.

All the words that really are necessary when receiving an award of any kind are the words "Thank you!" I was reminded of this recently while I was dining alone in a Miami Beach, Florida, restaurant. A child just nine years old was sitting at the next table with the entire family treating her to a dinner for her birthday. The waiters and waitresses even brought out a cake with nine candles on it flickering. The whole family broke into the "Happy Birthday" song and then applauded. Then, one of the group shouted, "Speech, speech!" There was more applause, followed by a long pause, and the young girl stood up, looked around with a big smile, said "Thank you," as she did a curtsy with a deep bow, and sat down. I was amused and impressed at the same time. I wondered why so many people fear saying a few words to accept an award or appreciation on a public occasion. This nine-year-old girl knew the answer.

Still, it usually is fitting for the recipient to dwell for a few moments on the meaning of the award and the gratitude or pride felt. Often the award has been earned through a long struggle and against great odds. Even at a retirement party there are so many interesting observations a person can make upon being heaped with praise, congratulations, and gifts. It might be appropriate, as well as inspiring, for fellow employees to hear you tell about the various bosses you had or the changes you've seen in the company over the years.

I heard one employee upon retirement tell the funniest things that happened over the years. On this occasion, I never heard a large group laugh so hard at what a speaker said. The insights of the speaker, as well as the experiences he related, were more entertaining than those told by many comedians.

Don't be afraid to tell your thoughts, reflections, feelings, and even experiences when you are the guest of honor or one of a number of people receiving awards.

When you are the only one being saluted and presented with an award, it's especially appropriate to take more time and go beyond the "Thank you!" Always express your deep appreciation and play yourself and your accomplishments down. As the late Dizzy Dean said, "If you did it, it isn't bragging!" However, modesty is called for, and credit should be given to those who helped you achieve the honor. Be lavish with your praise to colleagues or others who helped you in any way.

Ordinarily an acceptance speech would be no more than two or three minutes. However, there are exceptions to the rule. The main exception is when you are the guest of honor. It's expected that you will have more to say when you are in the spotlight. You might even be the featured speaker receiving a special award. Now you have an opportunity to inspire others. In short, always thank the donor of the award; give credit to all who helped you win the honor; tell what it means to you; and perhaps tell how you will use the award or where you will keep it; then give hearty thanks again.

Sometimes it might be best to be prepared with a fitting quotation, poem, or story. I heard one speaker who was given an award she had richly deserved say, "The Orientals have a saying, 'The hand that gives a gift retains some of the fragrance,' " and she added, "I will always remember all of you every time I see this trophy."

Another woman I know wrote her own poem for the occasion of an award she received—one she had worked hard to win. The poem consisted of only 10 or 12 lines but was written by her for her acceptance speech at the ceremony. I recall one line from that poem, "It's never too late to get things done." So don't overlook the power and impact of a poem, or a quotation, or even a short anecdote to express yourself.

My final warning for such speeches, or any speech, is to be prepared. Don't trust to the inspiration of the moment. Too frequently emotion blocks thinking, and words fail us.

HOW TO INTRODUCE SPEAKERS

The main thing to remember when you are introducing a speaker is that you are not the one giving the speech. It's your job to say a few kind things about the topic and the speaker to get the speaker off to a flying start. Brevity is essential. Enthusiasm is a necessary ingredient in introductions. After all, the only important thing is to tell the speaker's name with spirit, emphasis, and clarity.

Don't talk longer than one minute. A half a minute is usually just right. On rare occasions perhaps a longer introduction would be welcome. But brevity is usually the key to successful introductions. Speaking with spirit is also the only way to help the audience welcome the speaker enthusiastically and to help stimulate the speaker. Ed McMahon for years has provided the best example when he introduces Johnny Carson with a rousing, "Here's Johnny!" That's the kind of introduction I prefer: concise and with sparkle. Use a brief outline to save time and be accurate.

Put your ideas in any order you prefer, but always give the title of the talk clearly with emphasis. It might even be possible to cite a benefit the audience will gain by listening to the speaker. If the title is "How to Save Money on Your Income Tax," the benefit is obvious. But do try to highlight the importance of the subject to the audience. Give the audience a quotation, a statistic or a promise—some genuine fact to stir them to want to concentrate on the message.

The main objective of the speech of introduction, besides giving the title and the speaker's qualifications, is giving the speaker's name. By the way, you can use the speaker's name when you start the introduction, but you should repeat the name in the closing of the introduction also. Twice is alright, but don't keep using the name over and over in a brief introduction; the audience will get bored. Keep some suspense in it. Use phrases such as "our speaker . . . ," "our honored guest . . . ," and so on, rather than using the name repeatedly.

It is most appropriate, if not essential, to cite some of the speaker's qualifications to talk on the subject. Use the qualifications that support the speaker's right, experience, or authority to talk on the particular topic. Don't squeeze in all kinds of accomplishments that have nothing to do with the topic. Two or three solid qualifications are plenty. And keep it moving; keep it lively.

Finally, announce the speaker's first and last name vitally. Have the name written out on a card in front of you on the lectern so that you can glance at it at the last moment. Many introducers draw a blank at this climactic moment. Pause before giving the name. Look down at your notes, or glance to see that the speaker is ready.

When you do say the name, speak directly to the audience so that you will be talking into the microphone and the name will be heard clearly. Give the name with emphasis. Part the two names, The surname is the most important, so put more emphasis on the last name. Then start the applause.

A word of caution—don't turn to the speaker. Usually the speaker is seated to your side or even behind you. If you turn and announce the name while you are looking at the speaker, two things will happen: you will be telling the name to the one person who knows the name for sure; you will turn away from the microphone and no one will hear the speaker's name.

There are some things to avoid. Avoid giving trite, dull, or ungrammatical introductions. Think of creative, fresh, original introductions. Avoid saying such things as "without further ado" (that simply creates further ado) or "I present a speaker who needs no introduction." (Every human being craves appreciation.) Tell one nice thing about the speaker. Everybody who goes before an audience should be given an introduction. He or she needs it if the event is going to be handled professionally rather than amateurishly. Avoid saying, "well-qualified" and then not specifying why the speaker is qualified. Don't say "none other than" or "the one and only"; those two phrases are boring and trite. Tell one unique quality, accomplishment, or feature about the person instead.

Finally, do not close an introduction by saying, "I give you" or "Let's give him or her a hand." Both are grammatically wrong and dramatically dull. Both have been used incessantly by TV hosts, sports announcers, and introducers at conventions, dinners, lunches, and even breakfasts. Use of any of these clichés shows laziness and lack of originality.

It's fine to say, "I present . . . ," "Here is . . . ," "Let's welcome . . . ," or simply, "Now, our honored guest, Ruth Setterberg." Of course, it would be effective to make the final line more appropriate to the occasion, for example, "Let's have a rousing Teacher's Association welcome for the teacher of the year, Ruth Setterberg!" Then you can start the applause briskly.

Stay at the lectern until the speaker has come to the microphone. Just step aside and wait until he or she gets there. After your introduction it's proper to turn towards the speaker and say the speaker's name. Leave the lectern quickly once you have finished your introduction.

HOW TO READ A MANUSCRIPT

In our communication conscious society, people today want to hear speakers speak from the mind and the heart, not from a manuscript. Students in college and business people at work, as well as men and women attending community affairs, all make their wishes known. In a nutshell, it's "Don't read to me. Speak to me; tell me what you know." Even if the ideas on paper are the speaker's and not a ghostwriter's, listeners today want to know directly what *you* think, what *you* feel. They don't want someone to read to them.

Still, there will be occasions where it is necessary for you to read from a prepared script, perhaps at a press conference or a congressional inquiry. At such an important occasion you cannot risk saying the wrong thing. If you are asked to comment on radio or TV, you may even have to submit a script in advance. But otherwise, trust to an outline. Repeating Bishop Sheen's observation, "Never submit an active mind to a dead sheet of paper."

When you do have to use a manuscript, follow the rules for successful, professional manuscript reading. First, write the speech yourself if it's at all possible. This way you will have a genuine sincerity and a real familiarity with the material. Also, write the speech the way you speak, not in the form of long sentences of written communication. Dictate it in your usual speaking manner. Then have it typed verbatim on heavy bond paper. The typing should be the largest typewriter print possible. There are typewriters with large print that are best for this purpose. All of the typing should be in capital letters. Triple spacing should be used throughout the manuscript.

For today's audiences, the shorter the reading is, the better. Save long speeches for those times in which you don't have to read. Keep written speeches as short as possible. Of course, don't use a manuscript unless it's essential. Talk about what you know. Use an outline if you want but don't use a manuscript unless the situation demands it.

Now that you've got a well-written manuscript in spoken language, typed triple-spaced on bond paper in capital letters, you're ready to go to work. First read the speech through for meaning. As you read underline in red those passages that will warn you where emphasis is important. Make up your own markings for other cues; for example, for a longer than usual pause, I put two slash marks at the end of the sentence to remind me to pause longer. For quotations I use a bright color to show it is a quotation. I prefer having the words "quote" and "unquote" written right in the script, if it's important you say "quote" and "unquote." You might simply say that you're quoting and who said it. It's not always necessary to say "quote" and "unquote."

Once you've marked your manuscript for meaning, pauses, and emphasis, you're ready for a few practice rounds. It would be good to find an audience of one or two who would listen to you and could also give you some constructive feedback. This also will give you an incentive to practice looking up at the audience while you're reading. The idea is to know the manuscript material so well that you can look up most of the time. Practice is the answer.

If you can't find any listeners, use a videotape machine or at least an audio cassette recorder; either one of these will help you polish and perfect your reading. Try to make it sound spontaneous and real, rather than read. The only way this will happen is if you speak it through out loud as many times as possible. As you read, practice reading ahead as you pause so that you can look directly into the faces of your audience as you speak. Remember, the unforgivable fault is to neglect to look at the people you're talking to, and the only way to avoid this is to learn the material so well that you'll be able to look up frequently and see the audience.

I know from years of experience of reading manuscripts in radio and TV studios that you can look up most of the time if you know the material and if you have a desire to communicate directly with the members of the audience. A little practice will work wonders.

I can take young children who can read, give them a book they've never read before and teach them in 15 minutes or less to be looking up 90 percent of the time while they read the new book. I build in them a desire to communicate with their eyes and to look at their listeners. Even shy children improve to the point where in one session of a half hour or less they are looking up at least 50 percent of the time as they read. Parents can't believe it when they see the results.

Adults can learn this art of looking up while reading much faster than children. They can take a manuscript they've never seen before and look up 90 percent of the time if it has large print and good spacing. They can do this even with difficult, technical material.

All of the suggestions I made about preparation in Chapter 2 and organization in Chapter 3 apply to reading a manuscript as well. So reread those points to add to these guidelines for manuscript reading. Finally, be just as vital and animated when reading. Keep it lively. Keep it moving. The tendency is to go slower when you are reading and that's the last thing you should do when you are addressing an audience. It's necessary to speed up and have the proper pace in your talk to keep the audience's interest. This proper pace means you should read nonessential material faster (the buildup, the explanations) and essential material or technical ideas slower.

MAKING REPORTS PROFESSIONAL

Here are a few ideas about improving your method of making reports. It is safe to say that more people have been bored and more time has been wasted by long, dry, dull, reports given in a poor speaking style than any other type of speech.

Giving reports is more like reading manuscripts because most of them are text, rather than notes. Therefore, everything I've just written about reading manuscripts applies equally to reports.

The best report would be one that highlights information, not one that rehashes boring details. It's not necessary in most reports to give a detailed story. Narrow the report to important points.

A report should be specific, concise, and given in a spontaneous manner; that is, you should speak from an outline or from notes. Don't write or print out the report word for word and then read it. Give the essence, the key points, and the highlights in your best spontaneous manner and with the most spirit possible.

You'll be saving your own time as well as the audience's time if you stick to essentials only.

CHAPTER 11

How to Be Effective in Any Group

HOW TO SAVE TIME AND GET BETTER RESULTS IN MEETINGS

One of the biggest causes of wasted time is the staff meeting. Few of them accomplish their purpose because they are held without a definite established purpose or objective. An old anecdote about time consuming meetings is this: the secretary says to her boss at the end of an all-day conference, "How'd the conference go?" The boss replies, "O.K." The secretary inquires further, "What did you decide?" to which the boss retorts, "We decided to meet again tomorrow!"

There are usually two key problems with meetings: they are held too often and they are unproductive. We need guidelines on how often to hold meetings and ideas on how to improve the effectiveness of them.

Planning is the first step of good management. Meetings are a necessary forum for planning and discussing ideas, problems, budgets, and projects whether a group be large or small. Discussion brings people together. People understand through discussion, and this understanding provides motivation, commitment, and productivity. But how often should meetings be held?

There's a trend in major corporations to save time and money by holding meetings only as a last resort. The idea is to cope with information or problems in other ways if possible: face-to-face, by phone, by written communication, or by any other effective way.

Here's how to decide whether or not a meeting should be held. Hold a meeting only when you get a return on your investment of time and energy—the combined cost of all who attend. Translate this time and talent investment into a cost figure by taking the per-hour wage of individuals participating in the meetings. Weigh this cost for a half-day or an all-day meeting against the possible value of the results of the meeting. Some companies eliminated one-fourth to one-half of their meetings by using this method. Discovering the cost factor of your meetings will motivate you to start evaluating your situation.

Besides holding too many or unproductive meetings, other common problems are: too many people at a meeting, no agenda, starting late, unauthoritative leader, no control of discussion, no deadline, participants not prepared for the meeting.

Now, let's list some solutions. First, have an agenda and try to get it to all participants one day in advance. Encourage all involved to be prepared to discuss points listed on the agenda. People don't care unless they share. Next, limit the number of participants. For discussion purposes, 10 to 12 would be best; for problem solving or brainstorming, 16 to 20 would be best. The moderator should allow everyone to participate. Every member of the group should ask questions or comment. The moderator should be frank and explain the purpose of the meeting. What are the motives? Is the meeting to inform? Has a descision already been made? Is the meeting to get the ideas of those attending concerning the decision or decisions to be made?

Also, set time estimates for each portion of the meeting as well as for the entire meeting. Even set the estimate for a shorter time than you feel is necessary. It should keep the participants from rambling and the moderator from getting off the subject(s) of the agenda. The moderator should keep things moving.

Informal parliamentary procedure saves time and frustration. Investing in a gavel as a sign of authority will help to control the participants, to keep order, and to keep the discussion to relevant ideas. It is the moderator's job to keep the meeting on the topics and on time. A gavel is worth its weight in gold.

The moderator can save time by summarizing the discussion every once in a while, perhaps after each item on the agenda. This prevents repetition and keeps participants on the scheduled subjects, thereby saving a lot of time. Another way to do this is for the moderator to appoint a devil's advocate, an individual who will tell a participant when he or she goes off on a tangent. It is the moderator's job to integrate ideas or negotiate conflicts that arise. A leader should try to be a bridge-builder, connecting the ideas of all the participants. Sometimes it's necessary for the moderator to discipline people to listen. Sometimes this can be done by holding a 10-minute break. Or, as an alternative, the moderator can have a rule that no one can speak until he or she repeats in summary form what the previous speaker has just said.

HOW TO CONDUCT A CONFERENCE, A DISCUSSION, OR A MEETING

A dynamic leader of meetings and conferences must be expert at asking questions, listening, and controlling a group. Remember the sign on Lyndon Johnson's desk when he was in the Senate: "If you're talking, you aren't learning." To get others to communicate requires skill in questioning.

It is the ability to ask questions tactfully that puts a group at ease and also stimulates them to participate. And it's ability to question that helps a moderator find the common ground in disagreements, the reasons for objections, and the needs, problems, objectives, and convictions of the participants. Finally, it's this ability that fosters discussion, problem solving, and decision making. Expert questioning can also save time.

The four main types of questions are the overhead question, the direct question, the return question, and the relay question.

A question that the moderator asks of the whole group is an *overhead question*. It allows whoever has the answer to give it (calling on one individual may draw a blank and waste time). Overhead questions give everyone the opportunity to comment and help get a meeting started. If you were holding a meeting to discuss motivation, you might ask, "What is motivation?" And let as many people answer as want to. Overhead questions bring instant involvement and usually save a lot of time.

A *direct question* is used to call on a person for specific information or to involve someone who isn't participating. It's best to precede the question with the person's name to alert them to the question you'll ask, for example, "Marie, what is your experience with this type of person?" or "Jack, what do you suggest we might do about this situation?"

Moderators and chairpersons use *return* and *relay questions* to get others involved and to keep themselves from doing all the answering and most of the talking. A return question is used to bring out the ideas of others, namely the one asking the question. For example, when asked,

"Bob, how do you feel about this?" the moderator would say to the questioner, "Jim, what are your feelings?" or a relay question could be used and the moderator would ask the group, "How do the rest of you feel about this?"

Other types of questions are *open-ended* and *closed-ended* questions. Open-ended questions are ones that can't be answered in a few words (for instance, "Carmen, how did you get into the line of work you're in now?"). Closed-ended questions, on the other hand, can usually be answered in a word or two ("Bob, where were you born?"). Open-ended questions get people talking; closed-ended questions stimulate only a brief answer. Understanding the difference between open- and closed-ended questions can help you phrase questions that will motivate members of a meeting or conference to participate.

Here's an example of poor phrasing: "Why doesn't our government have a clear-cut foreign policy?" Instead, this question should be phrased, "Foreign policy is always complicated. What do you feel would be some essential positions our nation should have in formulating a clear-cut policy?" Instead of saying, "Do you agree with this?," the moderator should ask, "What is the thinking of the others on this point?"

Remember the suggestions already given on asking open-ended questions rather than closed-ended questions. Asking, "Do you feel this is fair?" will produce a "yes" or a "no" answer, but asking "How do you feel about this?" will usually encourage a detailed answer. The first is a closed-ended question, and the second is an open-ended question.

When you single out a certain individual for a question, preface the question with the person's name to get their attention immediately, for instance, "Bill, with your experience, what would you say about this situation?"

A skillful moderator redirects questions asked of himself or herself to give everyone a chance to participate. If you are asked, "How can we promote greater respect for authority among young people?," rather than answer yourself, you could return the question this way, "Joan, you work with the Juvenile Division of the Police Department; what do you say?" Everyone should participate. To foster participation, ask specific questions. To hold back those who dominate, limit each participant's time to two minutes. Ask the silent people to add to the discussion by offering their point of view.

A skillful moderator also will point out the middle ground of contradictions and arguments. It would be of great value for anyone who is going to preside over a meeting to obtain Robert's rules of order and to study them. Learn the proper parliamentary procedure and adapt it for informal use in business meetings and discussions. Follow a methodical order if it fits your meeting. This would include: call to order; minutes of previous meeting; reports of standing committees; reports of special committees; old business; new business; and adjournment.

All participants are potential speakers and all of them have the potential for leadership, but they need the opportunity to realize this. Your comments as a moderator must be phrased to command a hearing, to keep the members' interest and attention. The ideal is for you to keep listeners so interested that they will hear you out and listen to everyone else attentively.

Besides mastering the technique of questioning, the skillful chairperson or moderator must also be able to control the participants of any type of group: the larger the group is, the greater is the need for control. I've already included methods for saving time by exercising some controls of members of a meeting or discussion: use a gavel; have an agenda; set time limits for the individual topics and for the meeting; appoint a devil's advocate to keep things on time; take a break when the group gets restless; and have each person summarize the previous speaker's idea before offering a comment. There are also some excellent control techniques for specific problems that arise in meetings, conferences, discussions, and training sessions. Let's cover them one at a time.

People don't care unless they share, so your first goal is to see that everyone participates. Call on an individual by name, and try to make eye contact when asking a question as this produces results most of the time. Break the participants into small groups of two or three for discussion. Involve a quiet individual in making a report. Ask a question you know a person can answer because of expertise or knowledge that he or she possesses.

Another problem is handling the person who talks too much in a meeting. I find that the best way to handle this type of individual is to talk to the person during a break or outside the meeting room. I like to appoint "pace-setters" as assistants, who help me draw the others out. The group will often quiet down a dominator, but it's best to cope with the problem yourself first. You can always appoint the talkative individual to take notes on the meeting.

When a participant disagrees, allow the individual to explain why. Ask other members how they feel about that person's ideas. Of course, if the participant gets off the subject, thank him or her for any ideas, but draw the attention back to the agenda.

When individuals gripe about problems irrelevant to the subject at hand or bring up political, racial, or other personal topics not related to the meeting, rap the gavel and again repeat the subject under discussion. The gavel and the agenda are your best friends for doing a better job of moderating and doing it in far less time.

When participants are talking while you are, just stop talking suddenly and the silence will bring quick results. Or ask the individuals engaged in conversation if they have something they want to say to the group.

When an entire group is hostile, try to find out the reason for the hostility. It usually helps if you try to get open discussion on the cause of the inattention or uncooperativeness of the members. Even if it's a problem beyond your authority, just listening to them will often motivate them to participate.

When you are presiding and the meeting is called to discuss a proposition, decide ahead why you are for or against the proposition. Have one good reason at least and phrase it in a brief, colorful, easy-to-remember sentence. Use a key phrase to open your remarks. Tie your speech to the key phrase.

In presenting a point of view in a conference or discussion, use illustrations, since they will hold the interest of the participants and guarantee clarity. Also, they will provide emphasis. Use examples that support the reason you give for the idea or proposition.

Every member of a meeting or a discussion has a responsibility to participate. I like what George Bernard Shaw said about this: "We have no more right to drink in the conversation of others without contributing our own ideas as well, than we do to go into a store and take something without paying for it."

TIPS FOR PARTICIPATING IN MEETINGS AND DISCUSSIONS

The effectiveness of meetings, discussions, and conferences depends on the extent to which the resources of all members are utilized. Here are some guidelines for participants.

Speak your mind freely. Discussion is based on the exchange of ideas. No one else has your background, your experience, and your training so here's a chance to say what you think. Each of us has a responsibility to the group. Listening to others, however, is essential in order that you understand another person's point of view. Through questioning we can seek out the reasoning on which that person's view-point is based. Recall what I said earlier about identifying the evidence: Don't accept unsupported ideas, but remember that on almost every question there are several points of view.

Don't wait to speak until you're called on. If you wait, you may lose the opportunity to share your idea. Besides, speaking when you have the impulse may clarify the discussion or clear the way for action.

Try to keep your speeches to a minute or two at a time. Get to the point in as few words as possible. Allow others their chance. Also, it's a waste of time to argue about the ownership of ideas. Keep the team effort in mind and offer your ideas for the good of the group. Discussion is *not* a debate.

Seek clarification of what is being discussed so you understand. Ask questions when something isn't clear. Your contribution will be helpful only when you understand the ideas being discussed. And try to keep your remarks relevant. Don't digress. Don't repeat what has been covered already. In a sentence, act toward the moderator and members in the same way you want them to act towards you.

METHODS FOR INVOLVING PARTICIPANTS PRODUCTIVELY IN MEETINGS

Here are 10 reasons why people react favorably in meetings, discussions, or conferences. Human beings react favorably

1. when they have an interest in the project
2. when they see some benefit for themselves
3. when they know precisely what is expected of them and what they must do
4. when they respect, admire, or recognize the person making the request
5. when they understand why the request is being made
6. when they feel there is importance in what they're asked to do
7. when they know the time allowed and feel it's reasonable
8. when they feel they're being given the opportunity to cooperate
9. when they feel the request is sincere
10. when they feel the motives are honest.

Put these 10 ideas to the test as you prepare to conduct a meeting of any kind.

Preparations for a meeting include assigning someone to see that all necessary supplies are assembled along with equipment such as chairs, tables, microphones, visual aids, and other properties. This person also should make sure that water or coffee, tea, and soft-drinks are available to help ease the tension of participants and assure greater attention.

Speaking of visual aids, all of the ideas presented earlier about visual aids apply equally to meetings and conferences. The more visual aids you use to present your ideas, projects, and plans, the better will be your results. Again, about 85 percent of all we learn comes through our eyes. Experiment with flip charts, slides, overhead projectors, and flannel boards. Always keep a chalkboard of a good size available for anyone's use. Films, posters, and charts can add interest, variety, and clarity to any meeting.

A special type of meeting would be a creative thinking or brainstorming session. There's a rebirth of this type of creative problem solving for individuals or groups. Back in 1939, Alex F. Osborn, cofounder of Batten, Barton, Durstine and Osborn, started brainstorming in his company. The method worked so successfully that the firm appointed a vice president in charge of brainstorming. One year B.B.D.& O. offices held 297 separate brainstorming sessions in which they thought up over 15,000 ideas.

In recent years, brainstorming has been adapted in all types of industries for all kinds of problems. Charles Clark wrote a book titled *Brainstorming*, which is published by Doubleday, on the myriad of problems solved, ideas gained, and money and time saved through Osborn's method.

Experience shows that brainstorming is most productive when Osborn's four rules are faithfully followed:

1. Judicial judgment is ruled out. Criticism of ideas must be withheld until later.
2. "Free wheeling" is welcomed. The wilder the ideas are, the better; it's easier to tone down than to think up ideas.
3. Quantity is wanted. The greater the number of ideas participants present, the more the likelihood of good ones.
4. Combination and improvement are sought. In addition to contributing ideas of their own, participants should mention how suggestions of others could be turned into better ideas, or how two or more ideas could be combined into a still better idea.

A fifth rule should be added. Decide what action will be taken and who will take that action. And, as always, following up is wise management.

During the brainstorming session, one or two secretaries should write down all the ideas that come up. Having them written on a chalkboard or a flip chart for all to see aids the process. The entire technique centers around positive thinking, instead of saying what is wrong with the other person's idea and thereby stifling contributions.

Maybe you're wondering, "How can brainstorming be used?" It can be used anytime to develop ideas whether those ideas are to create or to improve something. Brainstorming works effectively when it is practiced alone or in a group of any size up to 30. I understand the social secretaries at the White House brainstorm for themes for parties and receptions, and these themes determine the type of decorations and the kinds of food ordered.

Brainstorming can be used with success for idea getting, problem solving, or decision making. If you have a problem or a decision to make, pose it clearly to the group and brainstorm for solutions. Follow the rules for achieving a complete process.

Few people realize that an international crisis was averted through use of the brainstorming technique by members of the U.S. State Department. North Korea released Commander Lloyd M. Bucher and the 82 members of the American ship *The Pueblo* after an 11 month struggle. The idea that finally proved acceptable came from a brainstorming session among senior State Department officials. Former Undersecretary of State Nicholas Katzenbach called it a "be imaginative and think of something else" kind of meeting. During the course of the meeting someone said "Well, here's one. We'll just tell them in advance what we think of their document and then we'll sign it and tell them why we're signing it." This idea worked.

If you are interested in creating a motto for your company or a campaign or project, or if you are trying to name a new product, get your people together and hold a creative brainstorming session, following the rules we've mentioned.

Of course, not all problems lend themselves to a brainstorming type of meeting. The problem may be too technical or too complex or not enough may be known about its causes. Therefore, we suggest a different type of meeting, a problem solving conference. A problem solving conference is the logical type of meeting to produce decisions that require a team, group, or committee to make. John Dewey's formula is our method: determine the problem; search out all the causes of the problem; offer all possible solutions; decide what is the best solution; and then decide specifically what is the first step to be taken to put this solution into action.

The first step is to determine the problem. As Kettering said, "A problem well-stated is already half-solved." There's an entire book on how to state the problem for a conference. The main emphasis is that a problem presented to the group in declarative form is better than one stated in question form. The reason is that a question arouses people to introduce arguments and this wastes time. For example, if you pose the question, "Should veterans of the Vietnam War be paid a bonus?," arguments and wrangles will start immediately and you may never get the group back to normal. However, if you state the same idea declaratively you will start the discussion in a rational, logical manner and save time, for example, "Veterans of the Vietnam War are having a hard time making ends meet and need a bonus." With inflation pinching everyone, it would be difficult to argue the point.

One more thought on stating the problem. It helps to think about it and try to state it in the clearest form possible. Just spending some time thinking about it can work wonders. I recall the woman who wrote to Ann Landers, the problem solver for readers of many newspapers. The writer wrote,

"Dear Ann, you helped me solve a problem without knowing it. Here's how: Yesterday I reached the end of my rope. I decided to write to you although I used to look down my nose at people who did. I stared at the paper for 20 minutes not knowing where to start. Finally, I sorted out all my hates and mental stumbling blocks in an effort to find a beginning for my letter.

Strangely enough, I began to view my problem in an orderly, rational manner. For the very first time I recognized the part I played in creating the problem. When I was finally able to accept my share of the responsibility I knew what the solution had to be. So bless you, Ann. This letter isn't worth sending perhaps, but the envelope is addressed and stamped, so I'm going to toss it in the mailbox."

Ann wrote back, "Your 'Problem' was the easiest one of the day. Thanks for mailing it."

So, thinking and writing out the problem could sometimes help you find the solution without a conference. The main point is, having thought out and phrased a problem well is already a giant step towards finding the solution.

Once you've settled on the wording of the problem, go on to the next step: search out all the causes of the problem. Ask participants to provide support or evidence for their findings. In fact, review all the criteria for holding effective meetings that we've already mentioned at the beginning of this chapter: have an agenda; get it out to others a day or two ahead of the conference; and ask members to bring in facts, ideas, and evidence for causes and solutions to the problem.

Once you've established all the possible causes of the problem, go on to the third step: call for all possible solutions. Again ask for any supporting data the individual has.

Remember to appoint a secretary to write down the ideas and after each step to review them. In a conference of this type, it saves time if you review the causes after every five or six suggestions are presented, and the same for solutions. This keeps everyone on the track and avoids repetition. It's important to record all the possible solutions so that you will have a record and will be able to review them for a vote on the best possible solution.

Once you have a tabulation of the preferences of the group for one or more possible solutions, work out the best phrasing of the solution or combination of solutions. Then, as a group, decide on the first action to be taken to implement this solution. Decide who will do it and set a date for when it will be done. Build in time for a follow-up to see that the solution has been implemented.

Cicero said, "To think is to live." Ideas change the world. The first step toward dynamic action is to acquire a habit of creative thinking. Any person who learns to think for herself or himself not only lives a fuller life but also becomes a greater asset to any organization to which she or he belongs.

One of the key principles of effective management is to keep the pipelines open. It should be helpful to look at meetings from still another perspective—the standpoint of organizational communication. There are two social systems—two communication systems—in every company, large or small. One is the *formal system* of communication, symbolized by the head. This system is the one by which management reaches objectives by plans, procedures, and policies. The other system of communication in every company is the *informal system*, symbolized by the heart. This system of communication is established by people to obtain satisfaction among themselves. It includes groups and clubs—everything from teams and union gatherings to coffee-breaks and the grapevine.

The less the formal system is satisfying, the more people identify with the informal system. The greater the gap between the two systems, the less effective is the organization.

To increase the organization's effectiveness, eliminate the conflicts that may exist between the formal and the informal systems. The first step, however, is to find out where there are conflicts or failure on management's part to communicate downward, formally. The question will arise, "How can we discover the conflicts?" The answer is to get the team or staff together and ask "How can we do a better job?" Then wait. Be silent. Be patient. Ask your people, "What can we do to improve communication?" "What can we do to improve our relationships?" and "What can we do to improve cooperation?"

It takes patience on your part as the manager if you're not accustomed to holding meetings of this kind and seeking the ideas of all parties. But if you do as I suggested, ideas will flow from the group.

Poor communication is a sign that something is wrong in an organization. In order to encourage good communication in your organization, management must support this principle: employees have a right to know anything that concerns them. The fact that they have this right is sometimes more important than the information itself.

Skill in questioning and listening has been emphasized earlier in this chapter. Here again I stress how necessary those two skills are to stimulate discussion and good ideas.

Perhaps the best success story on formal company communication with employees is the experiment of a major U.S. company in the 1970s. This multinational company owns plants around the country that manufacture food products. This company conducted a study of internal communications, which were considered ineffective. The study emphasized that good communication and favorable employee attitudes go hand in hand.

The top executives decided to conduct an experiment. The experiment was to hold a regular weekly meeting in some plants and not in others. It was noted that good communication means providing information employees want through the channels they prefer, namely through their immediate supervisors. So weekly 15-minute meetings were scheduled during working hours by every supervisor in the various plants. The supervisors would convey news, trends, changes, and any noteworthy items during the first half of the meetings, and the employees would request information and ask questions during the second half. The supervisors were held responsible for getting answers to any questions asked by the workers.

In those plants in which the weekly meetings were held, 81 percent of the employees said the company "tries to keep me informed," and 86 percent said the company "tries to give employees a fair deal." However, in plants in which communication was considered to be poor and no weekly meetings were held, only 34 percent of those interviewed said the company "tries to keep me informed," and only 58 percent said the company "tries to give employees a fair deal."

It is obvious from the vast difference in feelings of the personnel in this experiment that formal communication of information motivates employees and keeps morale high. It should be repeated that the employees' preferred source of communication is the immediate supervisor.

The primary objective of this program was to provide employees with information about what was going on in their specific work areas and in their plant. Also, employees had the opportunity weekly to say what was on their minds. The focus of the meetings was purely informational. The installment of the system was voluntary, but the success of the program encouraged managers to adopt the weekly meetings immediately.

Evaluation of the in-plant communication program has proved encouraging. The supervisors have become more involved with their people, and a better understanding has been reached. In fact, the attitudes of all participants have been changed. One manager reported,

> A feeling of frustration on the part of our people is being replaced by a happier mood. One man told me the other day, "We're getting information we've never had before. It's giving us a better understanding of how the mill operates. I already see a downward trend in the number of union grievances filed that deal with trivial issues."

Surveying the results, the company's board chairperson called a morning meeting of top management and quoted a series of "familiar phrases that summarize old and outdated attitudes." With each he proposed an alternative way. Some examples follow.

Familiar phrase: First-line supervisors are responsible only for task-oriented communications.

Alternative: First-line supervisors are the hourly workers' preferred channel for receiving information. We can meet this information demand through proper selection, training, and evaluation of supervisors and through adequate communication with them.

Familiar phrase: If we tell employees what's going on, it will leak out to our competitors.

Alternative: Our concern for security should not become an excuse to say nothing.

Familiar phrase: Yes, we communicate, and we do it in our own way. We know what our employees are thinking and what they want to know.

Alternative: These are sincere and honest beliefs, but, nevertheless, we need periodic, objective measurement of employee attitudes and information needs.

To summarize the successful experiment of this one company, here's the system. Each supervisor called the employees into a meeting for 15 minutes once a week on company time. The supervisor used half the time to provide information of interest to the subordinates, and then the employees used the other half of the time to ask questions, offer ideas, compliment, gripe, or just chat. The stunning results showed that the investment of time by the company payed off in happier employees, more motivated workers, and greatly increased productivity.

SETTING THE CLIMATE FOR GROUP COMMUNICATION

One final area for improving the effectiveness of managerial communication is the setting of a proper climate. Climate depends on the manager's style, self-image, and behavior.

Style is not what we say but what we are, and what you are determines climate. Our behavior should always confirm our words. One of the biggest blocks to communication is distrust. Trust is built by keeping one's word, admitting mistakes, and avoiding manipulation.

There are three levels of communication: *intracommunication, interpersonal,* and *public speaking.* In intracommunication we're assured of a sympathetic, responsive, intelligent audience because we talk to ourselves. We talk to ourselves silently all the time when we are making decisions about every move and action. The second level of communication, the interpersonal or person-to-person level, is one in which there is talk between two persons. It is important to note that when misunderstanding occurs on this level, usually the problem relates back to a breakdown in the first level. The third level of communicatoin is person-to-group communication, public speaking.

Self-image is so important, as suggested by breakdowns being traced back to the first level of communication. You need a positive opinion or image of yourself. How do you see yourself? How do others see you? What climate do you create—positive or negative? Are you easy to communicate with? Are you a willing listener? To what extent do you try to bring out the opposite viewpoint? To what extent do you tend to win or lose those with whom you deal? Are you fair to everyone? Answering these questions will provide you with solid information on where there might be weaknesses in your method of communicating that can be improved.

Behavioral communication can be compared to a mirror. People respond to you according to the image you present to them and will be comfortable with you insofar as you are comfortable with yourself. This is called *congruence:* being agreeable with or harmonious to yourself. If you like yourself, people will like you. We receive what we give, the self-fulfilling prophecy: we project an image and get this same image back. If we lack confidence, we're treated accordingly. No relationship is established if communication is difficult.

The new definition of communication is "Everything by which we extend ourself is communication." So let's master that idea of communication. Remember, behavior manifests belief. Our actions should match our words. Our example should support what we say.

In a football game (college or professional), 22 men, oblivious of the crowd, stop the game after every play long enough to hold two separate planning meetings, defensive and offensive. They analyze the situation, determine a course of action, assign every man a responsibility, and then carry out their plan. As soon as a play is run, they call another planning meeting, evaluate the results of the previous plan, analyze the situation, determine a course of action, assign responsibility, and then try to carry out the plan.

If it is important for a football team to hold about 80 such planning meetings during a game, it should be of equal importance for executives of a firm or corporation to hold meetings on a regular basis to plan, promote ideas, solve problems, and improve business. Communication is a problem solving tool. Through meetings we communicate to gain acceptance of ideas, to analyze problems, to reach decisions, to train, to delegate, and to sell.

If you follow the guidelines outlined in this chapter you will hold better meetings in less time. Remember the fast-paced, concise, tightly timed meetings a football team holds before every play. Keep all your meetings brief and to the point and you will save time and get better results.

Master Index of Professional Resource Material

INTRODUCTION

Many people are tempted to let serious world conditions depress them. Yet hopeless as these conditions seem, it's good to remind ourselves that history records many drab and somber scenes in the past also.

In 1809 the armies of Napoleon had conquered Europe and were poised to cross the channel into England when, for some inexplicable reason, Napoleon marched into Russia instead. So far as political and social stability went, conditions could hardly have been worse; the whole of western civilization was threatened, and humanity seemed to face only an age of oppression and tyranny. But in that very year babies were born also, among them Abraham Lincoln, William E. Gladstone, Cyrus H. McCormick, Charles Darwin, Felix Mendelssohn, and Lord Tennyson. These babies grew up and became leaders who changed not only the course of history but also our ideologies and mode of life.

Even today there will be bright young people who will make contributions that will right the wrongs of our society and create a new day of peace, goodwill, joy, and righteousness.

The following quotations, some inspirational, humorous or witty, others clever one-liners, are from men and women in all walks of life. Some are well known; others are not so well known. Many of the quotations are from unknown authors.

Effective speech-makers need solid speech material. The quotations that follow are meant to be a sample of sayings that can be used to highlight your ideas to audiences on different topics.

In the last half of this chapter I provide also some reprints of great speeches as a study of model speeches, exemplary openings and stirring closings.

GIVING / SHARING / THE ART OF UNSELFISHNESS

"He who loves doesn't consider the gift of the lover but rather the love of the giver." (Tilliche)

"The hand that gives someone a gift retains some of the fragrance."

LISTENING / SILENCE / DISCIPLINING THE TONGUE

"The ears don't work until the tongue has expired."
(For group meeting situations)

"The next best thing to brains is silence."

"Give every man thine ear, but few thy voice; Take each man's censure, but reserve thy judgement." (William Shakespeare—Hamlet)

"The aim of talk is to pave the way for silence." (Abraham Kaplan)

"There is a time to say nothing, and a time to say something, but there is not time to say everything."

"Those who know much usually say little, and those who say little, usually know much."

"Let no evil talk come out of your mouths." (Ephesians 4:29)

" . . . They found (Jesus) . . . sitting . . . listening . . . and asking them questions. . . ." (Matthew 2:46)

"If you don't say anything you won't be called on to repeat it." (Calvin Coolidge)

"There is nothing so like a wise man as a fool who holds his tongue." (St. Francis DeSales)

"The keenest mind—honed to the sharpest condition—is generally accompanied by a tongue that does the least cutting."

"There are two kinds of people who don't say much—those who are quiet and those who talk a lot."[*Marshalltown* (Iowa) *Times-Republican*]

"Bore: Someone who keeps talking when I want them to listen to me talk." (Ambrose Bierce)

"The art of listening needs its highest development in listening to oneself; our most important task is to develop an ear that can really hear what we're saying." (Sydney J. Harris)

"It's just as important to listen to someone with your eyes as with your ears." (Martin Buxbaum)

"Education is the ability to listen to almost anything without losing your temper or your self-confidence." (Robert Frost)

ENTHUSIASM

"Enthusiasm—the maker of friends—the maker of smiles—the producer of confidence—it cries to the world 'I've got what it takes.' It tells all men that your job is a swell job—the house you work for just suits you—the goods you have are the best."

"Years wrinkle the skin, but to give up enthusiasm wrinkles the soul. . . . You are as old as your doubt, your fear, your despair. The way to keep young is to keep your faith young. Keep your self-confidence young. Keep your hope young." (Dr. Luella F. Phelan)

"Enthusiasm is willing attention—a turning aside to see; without it we are blind, deaf and only half-know our world." (Michael Drury)

"Somewhere between wanting to remake the world and wanting to hide from it is a balance that permits intelligent adult enthusiasm—the God within which becomes the Art without. We no longer beg to know what life means—we furnish its meaning by being."

"To the degree that we deny the gift of life, we embrace death."

"Even though from now on I'm doomed to a life of deafness, I'll seize fate by the throat and not let it discourage me. I'll live life a thousandfold and continue to pursue and produce my art which for me there's no greater joy." (Beethoven)

HAPPINESS / CONTENTMENT /
PEACE OF MIND / FULFILLMENT

"You're only rich as the things you can do without." (Thoreau)

"Happiness doesn't depend on where or when we live, but how."

WORK / ACHIEVEMENT / USE OF TIME / ACTION

"You can't build a reputation on what you're going to do."(Henry Ford)

"Trying times are times for trying."

"Words are often as important as experience, because words make experience last." (William Norris)

"I never remember having felt tired from working, though idleness exhausts me completely." (Sherlock Holmes)

"The school with the highest tuition is the school of experience." (Alden Palmer)

"The art of using moderate abilities to advantage often brings greater results then actual brilliancy." (La Rochefoucauld)

"Where the willingness is great, the difficulties cannot be great." (Machiavelli)

"Diligence is the mother of good luck." (Benjamin Franklin)

"If a man love the labor of his trade, apart from any question of success or fame, the gods have called him." (R. L. Stevens)

"There is nothing truly valuable which can be purchased without pains or labor." (Joseph Addison)

"The trouble with opportunity is that it generally comes disguised as hard work."

"Those who make the worst use of their time most complain of its shortness." (Jean De La Bruyere)

GOALS / DIRECTION / PURPOSE / AIMS / OBJECTIVES

"The big struggle today is mankind's struggle to find the meaning of existence." (Camus)

"The man with a 'why' in his life can bear with almost any 'how.' " (Nietzsche)

LEARNING/GROWING/MATURING/SELF-DEVELOPMENT

"We'd all be wiser if empty heads growled like empty stomachs." (Arnold Glasgow)

"The taproot of enthusiasm is learning—it is sustained by the free play of our faculties."

"It is the man who is cool and collected, who is master of his countenance, his voice, his actions, his gestures, of every part, who can work with others at his best."

"The bird of time has but a little way to fly—and lo! The bird is on the wing."

"Our civilization is the sum of the knowledge and memories accumulated by the generations that have gone before us. We can only partake of it if we are able to make contact with ideas of these past generations. The only way to do this—and so become a 'cultured' person—is by reading." (André Maurois)

"There is no reason to make either books or education easy, any more than tennis or football is easy. Like sports, they require a certain amount of hard work and practice, and, like sports, they can be both a challenge and a delight." (Gilbert W. Chapman)

"What a shallow culture, after all, is that of one's first education. Superimpose a second on the first and again a third on the second. Break up the soil of your mind by ploughing it more than once and in different directions."

"Knowledge keeps no better than fish." (Alfred North Whitehead)

"We can't cross a bridge until we come to it; but I always like to lay down a pontoon ahead of time." (Bernard Baruch)

"Like food which leaves good flavors and taste in the mouth, the best in literature, art, music is that which flavors our lives with high enthusiasm, enjoyment and opens our eyes to the frailty in the world in which we live."

"A year from today you'll be the same man you are today—except for the people you meet and the books you read."

"At times to be uncertain in one's judgment is anything but a fault. Only he who at times feels uncertain in his judgment desires counsel, desires to go on learning, over and over again. And only one who keeps on learning is on the way to the fullness of truth." (Hans Margolius)

IDEAS / CREATIVITY

"We ought to spend more time 'wondering if' than 'doubting whether.' Wondering is the key to progress." (Gerald Bath)

CONQUERING FEAR, WORRY, AND FAILURE / SELF-IMAGE / HOPE / FAITH / CONFIDENCE

"We would worry less about what others think of us if we realize how seldom they do." (Ethel Barrett)

"A man is never down until he blames someone else." (Charles Jones)

"Only a fool has no fear—education consists of being afraid at the right time." (A. Fleming)

"How a man feels about himself is often more critical to his success than what he is objectively." (Dr. Harry Levinson)

"In giving, a man receives more than he gives, and the more is in proportion to the worth of the thing given." (George Macdonald)

"There's no courage unless you're scared; it's doing what you're afraid to do."

"The cost of all evil to come is the loss of confidence in one's own opinion and in oneself." (Boris Pasternak)

"The only enduring force in any civilization is its faith."

"Worry and trust cannot live in the same house. When worry is allowed to come in one door, trust walks out the other door; and worry stays until trust is invited in again, whereupon worry walks out." (R. G. LeTourneau)

"Worry is interest paid on trouble before it is due." (William Inge)

"The worst sorrows in life are not in its losses and misfortunes, but its fears." (A. C. Benson)

CONFORMITY / CHANGE / TRADITION

"The reasonable man adapts himself to the world; the unreasonable one persists in trying to adapt the world to himself. Therefore all progress depends on the unreasonable man." (George Bernard Shaw)

"Of all the forces acting in man, change is the most beneficial and most cruel."

"Perhaps the best thing about the future is that it only comes one day at a time."

CHARACTER BUILDING/VALUES/STANDARDS

"Decision of character will often give to an inferior mind command over a superior." (William Wert)

"Your personal charm and attractiveness is the result of something deep within which expresses itself in all you do or say."

"If you tell the truth you don't have to remember anything." (Mark Twain)

"Put this restriction on your pleasures: be cautious that they injure no being that lives." (John Zimmermann)

"A man's character is the reality of himself. His reputation is the opinion others have formed of him. Character is the substance, reputation is the shadow."

"Sow an act, and you reap a habit; sow a habit, and you reap a character; sow a character, and you reap a destiny." (G. D. Boardman)

"There is nothing so fatal to character as half-finished tasks."

"Men show their character in nothing more clearly than by what they think laughable."

"Character is like a tree, and reputation like its shadow. The shadow is what we think of it; the tree is the real thing." (Abraham Lincoln)

MISCELLANEOUS

"If at first you do succeed, try, try—not to be a bore." (Franklin Jones)

"He who throws dirt loses ground."

"Don't worry about swallowing pride occasionally. It nourishes self-respect and it's non-fattening."

(For the conference room wall) "Shall we do this definitely, clearly, sincerely, energetically, and above all immediately, or shall we continue to drift, talk and bicker and then do it?" (W. R. Sweatt)

"What a good thing Adam had. When he said a thing he knew nobody had said it before." (Mark Twain)

"One of our troubles today stems from the fact that too many adults, and not enough children, believe in Santa Claus." (Harry S. Truman)

"If you think the world is all wrong, remember that it contains people like you."

"When a man says money can do everything, that settles it; he hasn't any."

"The election isn't very far off when a candidate can recognize you across the street."

"A laugh is worth one hundred groans in any market." (Charles Lamb)

"I always prefer to believe the best of everybody; it saves so much time." (Rudyard Kipling)

"The ability to say no is perhaps the greatest gift a parent has." (Sam Levenson)

"Promises are like crying babies in a theater. They should be carried out at once." (Norman Vincent Peale)

"A man wrapped up in himself makes a mighty small package." (Walter Pitkin)

"Never let yesterday use up too much of today." (Will Rogers)

MODEL SPEECHES, EXEMPLARY OPENINGS, STIRRING CLOSINGS

President Lincoln's Immortal "Gettysburg Address," November 19, 1863.

Fourscore and seven years ago, our fathers brought forth upon this continent a new nation, conceived in liberty, and dedicated to the proposition that all men are created equal. Now we are engaged in a great civil war, testing whether that nation, or any nation so conceived and so dedicated, can long endure. We are met on a great battlefield of that war. We are met to dedicate a portion of it as the final resting place of those who here gave their lives that that nation might live. It is altogether fitting and proper that we should do this. But in a larger sense we cannot dedicate—we cannot consecrate—we cannot hallow this ground. The brave men, living and dead, who struggled here, have consecrated it far above our poor power to add or detract. The world will little note, nor long remember, what we say here. It is for us, the living, rather to be dedicated here to the unfinished work that they have thus far so nobly advanced. It is rather for us to be here dedicated to the great task remaining before us, that from these honored dead we take increased devotion to that cause for which they here gave the last full measure of devotion; that we here highly resolve that these dead shall not have died in vain; that this nation, under God, shall have a new birth of freedom, and that government of the people, by the people, for the people, shall not perish from the earth.

General Douglas MacArthur on April 19, 1951, tells a joint session of Congress that "old soldiers never die . . . ,"

Opening

Mr. President, Mr. Speaker, and distinguished members of the Congress: I stand at this rostrum with a sense of deep humility and great pride— humility in the wake of those great American architects of our history who have stood here before me, pride in the reflection that this forum of legislative debate represents human liberty in the purest form yet devised.

Here are centered the hopes and aspirations and faiths of the entire human race.

Closing

"Old Soldiers Fade Away"

I am closing my 52 years of military service. When I joined the army, even before the turn of the century, it was the fulfillment of all my boyish hopes and dreams. The world has turned over many times since I took the oath on the plain at West Point, and the hopes and dreams have long since vanished, but I still remember the refrain of one of the most popular ballads of that day which proclaimed most proudly that old soldiers never die; they just fade away. And, like the old soldier of that ballad, I now close my military career and just fade away, an old soldier who tried to do his duty as God gave him the right to see that duty. Goodbye.

General Douglas MacArthur returns to West Point May 12, 1962, to give his "Farewell to the Corps." (He used no text—not even notes—and this speech, given literally "from the heart," would have been lost to posterity had not someone arranged to record the speech on tape.)

Opening

As I was leaving the hotel this morning, a doorman asked me, "Where are you bound for, General?" And when I replied, "West Point," he remarked, "Beautiful place, have you ever been there before?"

No human being could fail to be deeply moved by such a tribute as this. (Thayer Award) Coming from a profession I have served so long and a people I have loved so well, it fills me with an emotion I cannot express. But this award is not intended primarily for a personality, but to symbolize a great moral code—the code of conduct and chivalry of those who guard this beloved land of culture and ancient descent.

Duty honor, country: Those three hallowed words reverently dictate what you ought to be, what you can be, what you will be.

Closing

The shadows are lengthening for me. The twilight is here. My days of old have vanished—tone and tint. They have gone glimmering through the dreams of things that were. Their memory is one of wonderous beauty, watered by tears and coaxed and caressed by the smiles of yesterday. I listen vainly, but with thirsty ear, for the witching melody of faint bugles blowing reveille, of far drums bearing the long roll.

In my dreams I hear again the crash of guns, the rattle of musketry, the strange, mournful mutter of the battlefield. But in the evening of my memory always I come back to West Point. Always there echoes and re-echoes: duty, honor, country.

Today marks my final roll call with you. But I want you to know that when I cross the river, my last conscious thoughts will be of the corps, and the corps, and the corps.

I bid you farewell.

Winston Churchill calls "Every Man to His Post," September, 1940.

Opening

When I said in the House of Commons the other day that I thought it improbable that the enemy's air attack in September could be more than three times as great as it was in August, I was not, of course, referring to barbarous attacks upon the civil population, but to the great air battle which is being fought out between our fighters and the German Air Force.

You will understand that whenever the weather is favorable, waves of German bombers, protected by fighters, often three or four hundred at a time, surge over this Island, especially the promontory of Kent, in the hope of attacking military and other objectives by daylight. However, they are met by our fighter squadrons and nearly always broken up; and their losses average three to one in machines and six to one in pilots.

This effort of the Germans to secure daylight mastery of the air over England is, of course, the crux of the whole war. So far it has failed conspicuously.

Closing

This is a time for everyone to stand together, and hold firm, as they are doing. I express my admiration for the exemplary manner in which all the Air Raid Precautions services of London are being discharged, especially the Fire Brigade, whose work has been so heavy and also dangerous. All the world that is still free marvels at the composure and fortitude with which the citizens of London are facing and surmounting the great ordeal to which they are subjected, the end of which or the severity of which cannot yet be foreseen.

It is a message of good cheer to our fighting Forces on the seas, in the air, and in our waiting Armies in all their posts and stations, that we send them from this capital city.

Winston Churchill coins the term "Iron Curtain" in a speech at Fulton, Missouri,
March 5, 1946.

Opening

A shadow has fallen upon the scenes so lately lighted by the Allied victory. Nobody knows what Soviet Russia and its Communist International Organization intends to do in the immediate future, or what are the limits, if any, to their expansive and proselytizing tendencies. I have a strong admiration and regard for the valiant Russian people and for my wartime comrade, Marshal Stalin. There is deep sympathy and good will in Britain—and I doubt not here also—toward the peoples of all the Russias and a resolve to persevere through many differences and rebuffs in establishing lasting friendships.

Closing

If we adhere faithfully to the Charter of the United Nations and walk forward in sedate and sober strength, seeking no one's land or treasure, seeking to lay no arbitrary control upon the thoughts of men; if all British moral and material forces and convictions are joined with your own in fraternal association, the highroads of the future will be clear, not only for us, but for all, not only for our time, but for a century to come.

"The Return of the Square by Charles H. Brower, President, Batten, Barton,
Durstine and Osborn, Inc., delivered in 1962.

Opening

Back in the days before the phrase "Going to His Eternal Rest" meant getting a job with the government, Mark Twain arrived in a small town where he was scheduled to make a talk. Noticing that his lecture was poorly billed, he stepped into a store and said:

"Good evening, friend—any entertainment here tonight to help a stranger while away his evening?"

The storekeeper straightened up, wiped his hands and said: "I expect there's going to be a lecture. I've been selling eggs all day."

There have been quite a few changes made since that day. Although the price of eggs may prohibit their use as indoor guided missiles, we have become so well to do as a nation that we have a guilt complex about it. Conformity is sweeping the country. And while more and more people want to get seats in the grandstand, fewer and fewer want to sweat it out down on the field. More and more youngsters who come in looking for jobs are asking, "What can you do for me?" rather than, "What can I do for you?" They want to discuss the extras.

Closing

We have, at least, the satisfaction of knowing that our problem is not new.

When Benjamin Franklin was told that "the war for independence was over, he said, "Say rather the war of the revolution is over—the war for independence has yet to be fought." And today—179 years later—the war for independence has still to be fought.

Index